13 to 19

Wendy Grant is a qualified hypnotherapist and psychotherapist. She lectures and writes on emotional and behavioural problems and the unconscious mind, and is the author of several bestselling books, including *Are You In Control?* and *Dare!* both published by Element.

By the same author

Dare!
Are You In Control?

13 *to* 19

A Parent's Guide to Understanding the Teenage Years

WENDY GRANT

E L E M E N T

Shaftesbury, Dorset ● Rockport, Massachusetts
Brisbane, Queensland

Text © Wendy Grant 1996
First published in Great Britain in 1996 by
Element Books Limited
Shaftesbury, Dorset SP7 8BP

Published in the USA in 1996 by
Element Books, Inc.
PO Box 830, Rockport, MA 01966

Published in Australia in 1996 by
Element Books Limited
for Jacaranda Wiley Limited
33 Park Road, Milton, Brisbane 4064

Cover design by Max Fairbrother
Illustrations by Alison Campbell
Text design by Roger Lightfoot
Typeset by Footnote Graphics
Printed and bound in Great Britain by Biddles Ltd. Guildford & King's Lynn.

British Library Cataloguing in Publication data available

Library of Congress Cataloging in Publication data available

ISBN 1–85230–862–1

Contents

Acknowledgements

I wish to thank my children, and all those young people who have shared their experiences with me, for making this book possible. My grateful thanks also to Tom Gregory for his computer expertise and patience – I couldn't have done it without you! Finally, my thanks to Julia McCutchen of Element Books for her original idea that grew into this book, and for her support and encouragement.

Introduction

When my first child was about four years of age, he asked me to do something for him one day, and I refused. Hands on hips he looked up at me. 'Just what *is* your job then?' he demanded. 'To make you entirely independent,' I replied, 'and then my job with you is finished.'

It was an immediate response, without any forethought, but this statement set me thinking: I realized that this was indeed my role as a caring parent. To do everything for my child, to make things too easy, to take away the struggles and sometimes the pain of learning, was not going to equip him to cope with life, neither would such behaviour on my part allow him to build a sense of self-worth.

During the first fourteen years of marriage, my husband and I had six children; we also cared for thirteen short-term foster children. They are now all grown up and have flown the nest and I reap the benefits of a large family, enjoying time playing with my seven grandchildren and sharing in the wonder of their development.

With all my experiences, and even after considering how life styles have changed, I still believe that those words I spoke to my first child apply as much today as they ever did.

It is incredible to think that the most important job most of us do – bringing up our families – is the one area in which we have little or no training. As our children move towards adulthood, the struggle to adjust, keep control, or to let go, is often daunting, exhausting, confusing and exasperating. But it need not be. Guiding our children through those years of change from child to adult can and should be one of the most rewarding experiences of parenting. For certain it will demand a great deal of understanding, insight, tolerance and learning.

When asked how old your children are, you may find when you mention they are approaching teenage that you are offered sympathy or a 'Heaven help you!' response. People assume it is going to be a struggle – some will have already been there and believe they *know* what you are in for. Well, I've been there too, and I know also that with a bit of inside know-how and a lot of love, you can build a strong foundation that will enable you not only to survive but to produce young adults of whom you can be immensely proud. They can become your best friends, people with whom you may converse as equals; they will help to keep you young, challenging and stimulating; they will share new ideas and perhaps even teach you some new ways of looking at things; they will add something to your life that is worth more than all the riches in the world.

I hope that as you read this book many things that have been bothering you will be made clear. I have attempted to give some ground rules that will help you to avoid conflict; tips on when to stand firm and when to let go; guidance in getting your priorities right; and advice on how to cope with situations that perhaps did not occur when you were that age.

The first time one of my sons stayed away from home all night I recall phoning the police who were extremely helpful but suggested I wait until morning to see if he returned. They were right; he did. Calmly explaining that he had run out of petrol for his moped and had spent the night at a friend's house, he could not understand why I was so upset. He thought involving the police had been an over-reaction on my part, and humiliating for him. I recall taking a deep breath and saying, 'You have to make allowances for me too, I've never been the mother of a teenager before. I don't know when to start worrying and when to trust that you can look after yourself.' This made sense to him and he was able to see my point of view.

There is going to be a first time for everything you experience too; reading this book will, I hope, help you to tackle the hurdles and make allowances for yourself as well as your offspring in this learning process.

In writing this book I have endeavoured not only to inform you but also to show you how you can achieve the positive desired results with your teenager.

Note: In my writing you will notice that I have alternated between the sexes – where this occurs the content applies equally to both (or either); where what I say refers *specifically* to one gender, it is obvious. Where I have used the plural 'parents' the content applies also to one parent.

Teenager–Parent Questionnaire

This has been designed to be used by you and your teenager. I hope, in sharing the answers, that it will help you to communicate better, identify your own feelings, and lead to a deeper mutual understanding.

You may find it helpful in introducing this to your teenager to say something like: 'I'm trying to learn how to be a good mum [or dad] to my teenage children. I've not been down this road since *I* was a teenager, and things have changed so much. Will you help me with this questionnaire?' After completing it you should discuss your answers with your offspring.

Questions for your teenager

- Do you believe your parents understand you?
- Do you find it hard to communicate your feelings?
- What do you consider are the most important qualities in a person (number in order of priority): Honesty; Determination; Confidence; Humour; Loyalty; Loving; Caring?
- On a scale of 1 (low) to 10 (high) how important do you believe are your looks?
- Do you believe education is important?
- What things do you least like about yourself?
- If you could, what would you like to change in your life?
- Do you believe that having materialistic things is important?
- Do you feel safe?

- Do you feel special?
- What makes you happy?
- What makes you really miserable?
- Do you believe you have a future?
- Do you feel in control of your life?
- Why do you think people take drugs?
- Do you believe they are harmful?
- What is the worst thing about being a teenager?
- What is the best thing about being a teenager?
- Do you think your parents interfere in things they shouldn't?
- What do you consider the worst thing about your parents?
- What do you consider is the best thing about your parents?

Questions for the parents

- Do you find it hard to communicate with your teenager?
- Do you worry about your teenager's future? His/her health? The influence of friends?
- Do you think he/she drinks too much?
- Do you worry that your teenager may experiment with drugs?
- Do you think he/she takes school work too seriously or not seriously enough? (ring one of these).
- Do you interfere sometimes when perhaps you shouldn't?
- Do you want to pass over more decisions and responsibilities to your teenager?
- What do you think are the most important qualities in a person (number in order of priority): Honesty; Determination; Confidence; Humour; Loyalty; Loving; Caring?
- What makes you miserable?
- What makes you happy?
- What is your biggest worry?
- Are you afraid of losing control?
- What do you plan to do when your teenager leaves home?
- Do you believe you have a future?
- What do you think is the worst thing about your teenager?
- What do you think is the best thing about your teenager?

1 Understanding What is Happening

WHERE DOES IT ALL START?

The best way to get things right is from the beginning. But where does life with an emerging adult start? How do you recognize the first signs, and what is the best way to communicate with your child who is starting the struggle for personal identity? 'I'm not a child any more!' can be a cry of frustration informing you that the way you are treating your son or daughter will no longer be tolerated.

With children of all ages it is important to be consistent. Children need to know where they stand and what is allowed. Although it may not be possible to enforce certain rules when you are out or in the presence of other people, they should not be allowed to get away with breaking rules and a quiet talk when you are alone is far more effective than pretending their bad behaviour doesn't matter. But please, try to avoid reprimanding them in front of others – and especially not in front of their friends. They will find this extremely humiliating and hard to forgive.

Your children may resent or oppose some of your rules but rules do, nevertheless, enable them to feel safe. They will know where they stand and, even if they never admit it, that is very comforting. 'Yes, that's okay when they are small,' you may say, 'but it is very different when they grow up.' Sure, the rules will change, but being consistent remains. When, for example, you

1

change the time they have to be home, you make it clear and – unless there is a very good reason – you adhere to those new times.

'The best thing about children is that when you put them to bed you know where they are,' a friend once told me. 'The problem is, when they reach adolescence you worry about whose bed they are in!'

Did it happen overnight? Did you see the signs of emerging independence? And when are you supposed to recognize your son or daughter is no longer a child? 'For goodness sake!' you may respond to the defiant child, 'you're only ten!' Yes! Fearful though it may sound, children of ten can already be going through the physiological changes that don't become outwardly apparent until, in the case of a daughter, she begins menstruation and there are signs of developing breasts and, in the case of a son, his voice begins to break and he starts to spend hours in the bathroom.

Outward signs are not necessarily a signal that the transition towards adolescence has begun. A child's body has been preparing itself for several years before you are likely to notice any changes. Little girls can start periods as early as nine or ten years. Although, in general, their development is some two years ahead of boys, little boys have penile erections from birth and, much sooner than most parents would ever imagine, they begin to compare themselves with other boys at school – they become sexually aware.

Before you start to panic, rest assured that all this is perfectly normal. The problem is that because parents are often not aware of the changes, they don't talk to their children early enough and can find themselves being overtaken by events.

Until the transition towards adolescence begins, you, as a parent, have been more or less in control. Of course you have had to deal with temper tantrums, sulks, defiance, a constant pushing against the limits, but you have made the rules and hopefully seen that they are respected, thus guiding your child into being a responsive thinking little person. You have learned to live together within the safety of the home environment. If you got things right, you will be firmly on the road to a good relationship that includes sharing and caring with mutual respect for each other's feelings. You will also have encouraged your child to do things that involve friends and school and which sometimes excluded your involvement. This, although you may not have consciously considered it at the time, will have been part of your initial training in preparing your child for independence.

Then, suddenly, it may seem that your opinions no longer count and there is rebellion against almost everything you suggest. The child seems not to want you in any part of his life and sees you as the enemy. 'You are spoiling my life!', 'You don't want me to be happy!', 'You just hate me!', are all words thrown at the parent to make you feel bad and hopefully persuade you to capitulate and let him do what he wants. Children learn very early on to cash in on the guilt game and to play one parent off against the other.

I once watched some baby gorillas at Jersey zoo investigating their surroundings. They stretched out one hand, picking at plants, sticks and insects, while the other hand kept a tight hold on their mother. When they moved in another direction they changed hands, but one hand always remained in contact with their mother. Our children are like that. They reach out for new experiences while part of them, whether they admit it or not, needs to know that you are there. One moment they may behave in an impressive adult manner, the next they can be rolling on the floor, giggling like two-year-olds.

These sudden jumps from child to adult and back again can be confusing. The important thing is to give your child time to make the transition without condemning seemingly irrational behaviour. Given time, they will make it, but reverting back to being a child is important and necessary during the first few years of growing into teens.

THE UNDERLYING MESSAGE

So you have recognized that your child has begun the rather bumpy path to adolescence; potentially worrying changes are taking place internally and externally. Change is frightening for most people and usually involves the unknown. If you absolutely know that your children will grow up getting good marks at school, settling for a career that will enable them to realize their dreams and be independent, that they will mix with friends of whom you approve, will not involve themselves in drugs, smoking or alcohol, and that they will not indulge in sex until they are married, then you can probably sit back and just let them get on with growing up. The problem is that you have fears – at first,

most of them probably imagined – and as you watch the development of your child these are likely to grow out of all proportion to what is actually happening.

When you find yourself confronting certain 'weird' hair styles, clothing, interests, and unusual friends, this doesn't mean your children are going to become dropouts, or criminals. They are making a statement: *This is who I want to be.* They are struggling to determine who they are, and usually there is a need for this to be different from the way they see their parents. This doesn't mean they think you are wrong; but that they can only establish their own identity by being different.

Many years ago we took the friend of one of my children on holiday with us. He had an impressive Mohican haircut that at that time was considered quite outrageous. Although we hadn't, until then, known him very well, he proved to be a very likeable, good humoured, helpful boy. When I got to know him better, I asked him why he chose that particular hair style. 'Well,' he admitted, 'when people look at my hair they don't see me.' It was his way of drawing attention away from himself. Outwardly confident, he was inwardly struggling very hard to establish his own identity.

More recently I had the opportunity to talk with a young man who has a number of very conspicuous tattoos on his body. 'I hate them,' he said. 'I only had them done because I thought people would think I was tough and leave me alone.'

Often a father sees his daughter's development as a threat – or it may arouse fears in him knowing *what men are like*. But gradually, we have to let go. We have to learn to trust that our children won't make big mistakes and, no matter what, they need to know that they have our support and unconditional love. No matter how far they step outside your idea of what is proper, they need to know you will still be there for them. It is important for all children to understand clearly that although you may not always *like* their behaviour, you still love them.

It is very important and helpful to examine your own feelings before reacting to any drastic changes in your child's behaviour or appearance. So often, what we are most concerned about is that they show us up and give us a bad name. We see their behaviour as an indicator of the way we have brought them up – and *What will people think?* The earlier you can recognize when your feelings are defensive or protective of yourself and your own values, the easier it will be to adjust to your emerging young adult. Also, should your teenager change and conform to your ideas about what looks right, don't draw attention to him by using words of praise in front of others; he is likely to hate this and may never wear those clothes again.

Of course, not all children are going to rebel; some will continue to fit into the pattern set for them by the parents. We may look in wonder at the child who seems to fulfil all of the parents' expectations, but in reality many of these children have a very deep-rooted problem – *fear.*

In my work as a psychotherapist I meet these people in later life. Often they have never had a romantic encounter of any kind, and they stay at home, continuing to fulfil their parents' expectations. Then, when the parents die, they find themselves completely without direction or purpose. They can feel very bitter or resentful, realizing that they have given up everything in order to please their parents or to fulfil what they were taught to believe was their duty.

You can do all that is within your power for your child only to have it thrown back in your face when, as an adult, he recognizes the control and limitations of such devotion on his own life.

With some children – especially those who are shy and self-conscious – it is quite easy to persuade them not to venture out into the world, but it is cruel and selfish, and also unnatural, to limit their lives in this way. We need to encourage independence – it is one of the greatest gifts we can give to our children.

By now you can see that change and rebellion are a natural part of growth; rather than restricting or stifling this reaching out for new experiences, you should try to direct the young person along a positive path.

Get involved. For example, if your child suddenly starts playing modern music at full blast, ask to listen, be interested, and then by all means request the volume to be turned down. Your interest will get a much more positive response than if the child believes you just hate anything he plays.

Discussing this recently with my youngest son he said that this was one area where I had failed. He would have so liked someone to be there watching him play in sports matches. Although he now understands that at that time my husband had died and I had to work to support us, when he was between twelve and sixteen it really made him feel sad and left out when other boys had their Dads cheering them on. In cases like this, Mum is perhaps a poor substitute, but I should have made the effort. I could have encouraged and listened to him talking about the match afterwards. I didn't even think about it – I ought to have known better.

It is important for you to recognize that some of your feelings towards your teenager may be something more than concern for him. You need, from time to time, to examine your underlying feelings. Here are a few pointers for you to consider:

- Are you fighting against changes in your child because it makes you feel old?
- Are you feeling resentment for some reason?
- Are you jealous of your child's boyfriend or girlfriend?
- Are you experiencing guilt and thus adopting a defensive position?
- Are you envious of the freedom and opportunities your child has that you never had?
- Are you worried what other people may think or say about the way your child is dressing or behaving?
- Are you afraid of criticism?
- Are you afraid to let go?
- Are you afraid for their future or your own?
- Are you trying to get them to fulfil your own unfulfilled dreams?

PART OF THE FAMILY

It is important, as children move into adolescence, that they still feel part of the family. Once they experience isolation they are going to spend either more time in their bedroom or out with friends. If you don't seem to understand them, or take time to interest yourself in what they are doing, they will quite naturally come to believe that you no longer care.

- Do you know what kind of books, films, sport, hobbies, interest your children?
- Do you know what makes them laugh?
- Do you know who they admire and wish to emulate?
- Do you know what subjects they hate at school and why?
- Do you know what makes them afraid?
- Do you know what they would really like to do if they had the courage?

Listen to your children. Find out what they like talking about, and be interested. You may not like the subjects, hobbies, styles and personalities that they choose, but you should be interested in finding out why they appreciate them. But do avoid being patronizing or intruding into their privacy.

If you have children whose ages span a number of years, it isn't always easy to think of something you can do as a family. With twelve years separating my eldest from my youngest, I had to address this problem. I have always felt that family was very important, and while recognizing that at times they would be involved in different activities, I still believed that it was important for us to do things together. One of the activities we did share was to meet on Friday nights at the local swimming pool. The older ones felt good teaching the smaller members of the family, and they had no difficulty in discovering a dozen different ways of having fun together in the water. Afterwards we would go to the local café, where we treated ourselves to a sit-down meal. It didn't cost a fortune, no one felt embarrassed, no one was put down, and it remains one of my fondest memories.

Table tennis, exploring the countryside, riding, darts, archery and board games were other activities we could share.

Eating together, at least once a day, is another way of family sharing. This should involve discussion about good news as well as the opportunity to air grievances. It is one time in the day when television should be switched off and the meal – and cook! – given the respect they deserve. If work, out-of-school activities or other commitments mean that you cannot sit down to dinner as a family, try to set aside some other time for being together and talking.

You may find that when your teenager has school friends around, she does not want to be seen as part of the family; she actually feels embarrassed. This is not because you are at fault, but that she sees this as an indicator that she is still a child.

A friend of mine went shopping one Saturday with her fourteen-year-old son. Suddenly she became aware that his face had reddened and he was hanging back. It was then she saw two lads from his school and realized how uncomfortable he was feeling being seen shopping with his mother. She never asked him to go with her again.

Growing up can be painful, confusing, embarrassing, and sometimes terrifying.

DEALING WITH THE THREE Rs

In considering some of the underlying problems young people have to deal with, it is worth taking a look at what I call 'Fear of the Three Rs': *Fear of ridicule. Fear of rejection. Fear of reprisals.*

Ridicule

Of all the things that may affect a person's sense of self-esteem, ridicule comes top of the list. This is never more so than when your body is changing shape, your voice suddenly becomes alien, you don't know how to behave any more, and everything you do seems to be the butt for ridicule both inside the family and out.

I see clients of all ages who are struggling to overcome self-doubt and lack of confidence, and who have often become too afraid to try anything new. When I ask, 'Do you know when this started?' the response is most often, 'When I was at school . . .' Someone, often a teacher, had made them look ridiculous in front of the other children. Scorn, mockery, comparison, trying to urge them to do better in front of others, can all have quite disastrous results. You can perhaps recall an incident when you were made to feel conspicuous. Confidence can crumble in seconds, and it takes a great deal of courage to convince yourself that what has happened is an isolated case and does not have to affect the way you view yourself as a human being. Emotions are not rational and, unfortunately, are usually far more powerful than logic.

Many people deal with self-consciousness by avoidance. It may work, but is not the best way of dealing with the problem. Also, you cannot be sure that you will never need to face people in the situations that you have been avoiding.

Why is ridicule so painful? When all attention is turned on you – especially when you are very young – you are made to feel vulnerable. You feel threatened. This leads to self-doubt: *There must be something wrong with me.* Almost always this is not the case; the problem lies with the person who has put you in that position. When you are young it is usually impossible to rationalize in this way, and it is often still very difficult when you are a mature adult.

Of course, feeling ridiculous does not have to be the result of someone else's treatment of you: your pants suddenly falling down around your ankles, saying something entirely out of place, singing on when everyone else has stopped, discovering you have arrived at a function dressed completely differently to everyone else – all these can cause deep embarrassment, rosy cheeks, and the wish to drop into a hole in the ground and disappear. So when you see your son walking down the stairs in the most outlandish clothing, try to hold your tongue – he may need to dress this way to be part of the crowd with whom he hangs out. And being part of this group makes him feel safe and accepted. At moments like this, what his contemporaries think and say is more important than your somewhat outmoded idea of dress.

When your son has his head shaved save for a bunch of curls on the top of his skull, three rings through his nose and a tattoo on his neck, it is difficult to say nothing. Perhaps you know that is why he can't get a job – his very appearance prejudices people against him. At the right moment, you may be able to point this out and suggest he keeps some of his rather unusual styles for his social life: he will see that judging people by the way they dress is unfair, but we have to make a judgement of some kind, and often all we have to go on at first is the way people present themselves to us. When he sees others being employed and still he gets no further than the first interview, he will eventually come to realize that he needs to make some changes.

Learning to compromise is something we all have to do in certain areas of life. However, this has to happen when your teenager is ready, and not when *you* think he should 'sort himself out'. If he has experienced a good deal of ridicule from his parents and family, and if he feels they are all waiting to pounce on him with *I told you so*, it may be very difficult for him to climb down and admit that you were right. He may feel forced to stay with that image long after he has outgrown it. When he does change, resist telling him how much nicer he looks now he is conforming to what he may still see as *your* idea of what is acceptable.

If your child does suffer from a lack of confidence and poor self-esteem, and he can recognize when and how it started, the following exercise will help to undo the negative responses. It may be helpful to explain to him that many sports people use these, or similar visualization techniques, to improve confidence and performance (often known as autogenic training) with very positive results. This is sometimes called self-hypnosis, but as there are so many misunderstandings about hypnosis it is easier, and quite correct, to describe it as learning to achieve that level of mental relaxation when we are at our most receptive to positive suggestion – this is known as **alpha level**.

Following up this exercise with positive visualization helps to replace negative internal images with ones that begin to make us feel better about ourselves. It is very hard to change a negative attitude which has been reinforced for years with such thoughts as: *I'm useless. Anybody can do it better than I can. I'll only get it wrong. No one in their right mind wants to be bothered with me. I'm a failure. Everyone will laugh at me.* Encourage your teenager to use positive statements. And then – with practice – he will be able to achieve almost any goal. It is best to start with easily accessible goals which, with a little effort, can be soon achieved. This will help him build a new belief in himself.

This exercise may be put on an audio cassette, or read aloud by someone while the listener relaxes and responds. Your teenager may choose to do this exercise on his own. He will, in this case, need to read quietly through it first and then to relax and follow through the instructions given. (You can, of course, use it yourself!)

For those sitting examinations, this exercise plus positive visualization is a very useful asset. I recall asking one of my sons if he would like to borrow a self-hypnosis cassette to help him during exam time. No, he told me, he didn't need to, thanks. I was amused to find him a few days later lying on his bed using another cassette to help improve his game of snooker!

Exercise 1 – Building confidence

1 Take ten minutes off from doing anything else and relax, either on your bed or in an armchair. Close your eyes and breathe deeply for a few minutes. Concentrate on the feelings you experience as you physically let go and relax. Start with

your toes and feet ... now your leg muscles ... your stomach muscles ... your chest ... Notice how the rhythm of your breathing slows down as you relax ... Now let all of those tiny muscles in your head relax. Allow a calm, peaceful expression to spread across your face. Feel your jaw relax ... Imagine all the stress and tension in your head, your neck, your shoulders, flowing away down through your arms and out through the tips of your fingers ...

2 Enjoy this relaxed feeling for a few minutes, and then picture a situation in which you do not feel very confident. This may be speaking up in front of others; asserting yourself in a shop or café where you have been overlooked; walking into a room full of people you do not know very well; sitting an examination.

   Now ask yourself: Where did this lack of confidence start? Perhaps at some time you were made to feel stupid or embarrassed in front of others. Or there may be a person in your life who is intimidating or very critical. Why do you think you feel unsure of yourself? Are you perhaps worried about what people will think or say about you? Are you afraid of failure?

3 If you can remember where you were when you first experienced that bad feeling, imagine now that you are watching it on a video at home. If you don't know what has caused it, simply picture a situation that results in the worst of those feelings. As you watch the picture on the screen, try to understand why you responded in the way you did. After you have watched the picture for a few moments, imagine pressing the controls and running the whole thing backwards – it is just as if you are undoing the situation.

4 Now take the video out of the machine and dispose of it in whatever way seems appropriate to you: you may burn it on a bonfire, throw it in the trash can, smash it with a hammer.

5 Imagine now that on the TV is a picture of you in the future. See yourself in that situation you visualized at the beginning of this exercise, only now you are confident and smiling. You feel sure of yourself and your new responses. Play around with

this picture until it feels really good ... take your time. When it looks and feels right, imagine slipping into that picture and trying out the new behaviour.

6 Say quietly to yourself, *I can do it. I'm feeling fine. It feels good to be me.*

7 Make one hand into a fist and for a moment hold onto that good feeling. Relax your hand and then gently open your eyes. Remember to use this new behaviour as soon as the opportunity arises.

Note: By deliberately making your hand into a fist in this way it acts as a restimulation of those good feelings and helps strengthen them.

Try to repeat this exercise on a daily basis until positive responses are experienced.

Rejection

At a very early age we learn that rejection is painful. To feel safe we need to know that we belong; it becomes part of our survival kit. When either parent threatens to withdraw love or to leave home, fear of rejection becomes a powerful motivator (or inhibitor) and is an effective way of keeping control. Most parents drop into this threat mode occasionally and, although it is rarely meant, a small child doesn't know that. *I can't stand you near me when you* ... or *Go to your room, I don't want you when you're snivelling like that* or *How can I love you when you do such naughty things?* Although not intended, the threat of rejection is there.

Bullying at home or at school is another form of rejection – the child feels different, unacceptable, pushed out, unwanted. Self-doubt creeps in and the child's belief that there must be something wrong with her is reinforced.

The teenager has a tremendous conflict to resolve: to be accepted by her peers she needs to fit in – to be like them; and at the same time she often finds herself having to conform to another set of values to be accepted at home. Whereas the early teens is when being one of the crowd is so important, the latter part is, hopefully, when the child begins to feel confident enough to be an individual with her own opinions, likes and dislikes. However, this healthy development can only come about if the teenager has had time to work her way through the process; she has to build sufficient confidence to be who she really is, and not to feel that she must fulfil a role dictated by others.

Failing exams or a job interview, having no steady boy friend or girl friend, can all be seen as forms of rejection. It really is very important to guide and encourage your children to participate in sport, hobbies or in interests where they will succeed. Everyone is good at doing something – when we pursue those things we enjoy, we usually become good at them. Young people who find it difficult to communicate may, for example, have an empathy with animals; through this interest they will meet other animal lovers, and having a common interest makes it so much easier for them to talk and make friends.

Although it is not always possible to choose as a career something we love, it can usually be pursued outside work or study time. By working for a charity, club, association or organization, we can always find a way to follow our interests. This applies as much to adolescents as adults.

Because young people do usually have to spend a great deal of their spare time studying, other areas of their lives can easily be neglected. It is important for them to take exercise of some kind. Whether this is with family or friends, it should be encouraged. A break from studying allows the brain to rest, and results in more creative thought emerging when they return to their books.

One of the most painful areas of rejection is when a young romance comes to an end. Unless termination of a close friendship is mutual, one of the pair is going to find getting over those feelings very hard. Earlier experiences of rejection will play an important part in how they cope later. (Relationships are covered in detail in Chapter 7.)

Reprisals

Worrying about what will happen to them if they take certain action can totally inhibit a young person's life. They may long to move from one group of friends to another, change the subjects they have chosen to study, move to a different school, terminate a close relationship, alter their appearance ... the list is endless. But fear of what may happen to them if they take that step – though often imagined – may totally control their lives.

In many cases the young person may have had an experience much earlier in life that has left emotional scars. It seems almost a natural response when a child is young and controlled by authoritative figures to believe that everything bad that happens is his own fault.

A teenager who spends a lot of time studying may become the butt for teasing or bullying, or may find himself completely ostracized by the rest of the class. The sad truth is that being different does often cause adverse behaviour from others.

Unless the adolescent is sure of himself, being adventurous is something he may have a secret longing for, but never dares to voice in case you push him in that direction. New trends and styles would never come into being if some people did not dare to be different. Many pop groups simply fade back into the unknown, often ridiculed by those who heard them, but there are still those who do make a successful career by setting a new image and new style with the songs and music they play.

If your child wants to try something different but expresses fear, suggest that he asks himself these two questions: *What is the worst thing that can happen if I do this?* and *How will I feel when I succeed?*

Where you see your teenager attempting a behaviour that does not seem in any way to make him happy or is out of character, it is worth investigating whether there are deeper reasons for his behaviour or rebellion.

Of course it is important to be realistic and at the same time to focus on the best outcome from our actions. This is the road to success. Imagined failure is never going to allow the freedom of thought and action that progress requires. Encouraging your child to take risks, to cope with change, to see difficulties as challenges, will all help him to grow up free of the invisible shackles caused by the nagging doubt – *What will happen to me if things go wrong?*

Reprisals are seen as a kind of punishment or a retaliation of some kind. *People will think I'm stupid. My friends won't like me, they will laugh at me, think I'm a swot, never invite me again.* The reaction to certain types of behaviour does not have to be physical: reprisals taking the form of mental torture are a far more powerful deterrent.

SUMMING UP

This chapter has been designed to give you a general insight into what is happening to your child as he or she makes the challenging journey to adulthood. Ideally, if you can gain understanding before that journey really takes off, you will be better equipped to handle the varied aspects of adolescence as they arise.

It is impossible to cover every event and problem you may encounter, but I hope to give you a foundation from which to work and build your own satisfactory relationship with your teenage children. I have tried to deal with the challenges, insights and the know-hows of living with an adolescent in the order in which they are most likely to arise.

Remember, you are not perfect; you have probably never been along this road before. Expect to make some mistakes; there will probably be moments when you feel everything you do is wrong, and your teenager seems like an alien.

The reassuring news is that most young people reach maturity without setting the house on fire, joining the Mafia, ending up on drugs, or becoming teenage parents. In fact, statistics reveal

that more than 70 per cent of children – after they have strug-
gled to establish their own identity – end up very much like
their parents. They settle down in steady jobs with a permanent
roof over their heads, have a family, enjoy the same kind of
holidays and food they once spurned, and dress in remarkably
conventional clothing.

It all just takes time, plus a good sense of humour, tolerance,
firmness, and the kind of love only someone who has had the
privilege of bringing up children can give.

2   Puberty and the Changing Image

WHAT IS HAPPENING TO ME?

Do you remember how you felt when your own body began to change? I can recall feeling extremely angry at what I saw as these new, unwanted, limitations to my life. Most of all I hated having to cope with menstruation every single month, and with everybody knowing when I had to be excused from taking swimming classes – in my day school rules did not permit us to use the public swimming baths at such times. *Everybody*, I used to think miserably, would know. It was the one time when attending a mixed sex school became a disadvantage.

At first I used to tell myself that one in four women must be having a period just like me, but it didn't console me one little bit. At twelve I didn't want to be able to have a baby, but I did desperately want to be in the netball team, run for the school, and go off camping without any physical restrictions. Breasts were another inconvenience – they got in the way and they were definitely *not* an asset if you liked horse riding or being athletic!

The first period usually begins about a year after the first physical signs of change. If you stay aware, you will notice your daughter's young body begin to change shape – most noticeably the forming of breasts. But some girls do not develop much in this area (or not until later), and so it is important that your daughter does know what to expect and how to cope with a period if one should start when you are not around; don't put her in the embarrassing position of not knowing what to do. Usually there is a teacher she can go to if this happens at school. Tell her this, and if necessary find out who is the best person she can confide in when away from home.

You will need to discuss the kind of sanitary protection that is best suited to your daughter. Different cultures and religious beliefs are relevant here – many people believe that internal protection in the form of tampons will harm, take away virginity, or create infections – applied properly none of this is so. Help your daughter learn how to use pads or tampons hygienically and safely, advise how often she will need to replace them and how to dispose of them.

Although fathers do not usually get involved in all this, they need to be told what is going on; menstruation should *never* be a topic for jokes or innuendoes, but should be a very personal thing that is respected at all times. A special hug from dad, *for my lovely daughter now you are growing up*, will tell her that you care for and love her just the same. In time she will learn to handle her menstrual cycle discreetly, but to start with being made to feel special will be a tremendous ego boost that she probably desperately needs. I have known women who still, in this age, view menstruation as a time of being unclean and isolate themselves with shame. This is particularly true in some religions and tribes.

Explain to your daughter in simple words exactly what is happening when a period occurs. Assure her that it is natural and, if necessary, that she is not going to bleed to death (some girls really do think they will). Tell her this blood is not *bad blood*, but the lining of the womb which has grown in order to nurture a baby, but as it isn't needed yet it separates and leaves the body.

At this time her breasts may become tender, she may put on weight (which she will hate), experience some fluid retention, and feel irritable. If this does happen, tell her it will soon pass, but show a little extra love and understanding.

Although periods generally go in approximately 28-day cycles, they may be erratic during the first year. This is also quite normal and will usually sort itself out. However, if you or your daughter are worried, do go and talk to a doctor; she will probably find it easier to speak to a woman doctor at this time. You may have a women's health clinic in your area, or an equivalent medical advisory body. Reassurance from a professional person will be enormously helpful.

It is advisable to broach the subject of a bra before, as in my case, the sports mistress took me on one side and told me to go home and tell my mother to do something about my chest! A shopping trip that also includes purchasing a nice top can make girls feel good about this change in appearance as well as status.

We do need to talk to our children before changes start to happen; it is so much easier to cope when you are forewarned. Of course, very young children have a natural curiosity, and if you have responded to this in a truthful way you will have made the path easier for both you and your children.

Emerging young adults of both sexes have a lot to cope with; it is no wonder they get resentful, angry, frustrated, confused. The problem is that they may be either way behind or way in front of other friends in their development. Because things don't usually happen in a balanced manner, they are going to feel, for a couple of years, as if they are living in an alien body; worse still, they may believe that they alone have their problem.

Traditionally, it has been father who explains bodily changes to his son and mother who does so with the daughter. This can, however, immediately create barriers and cause embarrassment later. Letting your child know that you are both aware when physical changes occur is advisable, and then if, for example, your daughter is out with Dad and a period arrives ahead of schedule she will find it easy to ask for the help she needs.

I remember a very funny incident that happened in our family of three daughters where all conversation on sex and reproduction was left to mother. My eldest sister, who had advanced to using internal sanitary protection (this was a fairly new and adventurous step in the 1940s), had left a tampon on the shelf next to the open bathroom window and the wind had blown it down into the garden below. My father, on finding this, brought it into the house and told my mother: 'I found this outside, I think it must be some kind of firework.' He had no idea what it was.

Life does sometimes seem to play cruel tricks on us: just when a girl or boy needs to feel at their best, they have to cope with awkward changes, often becoming incredibly clumsy, blushing painfully, getting spots and other skin problems, and finding themselves with a tubby body before it reaches its mature shape. In addition to this, a girl may experience period pains or cramps in the stomach muscles. They used to tell me that all this would end when I had my first child – *it didn't*. But I did find that physical exercise helped, even though I often didn't feel like it. Giving myself a treat did provide some compensation. This is perhaps where some women and girls start eating chocolate; it feels like comfort, but the end results – possible skin problems and weight gain – don't help. As a parent there are things you can do to help your teenager through this difficult time.

- Provide Vitamin B6 – this really does help with period pains and cramps
- Get your teenager interested in helping you to choose and prepare healthy meals
- Have alternatives to chocolate available – health food shops offer many. Also have fresh fruit and salad pieces prepared and kept in the fridge (slices of carrot, celery, cucumber, etc)
- Encourage participation in sport or physical activities
- Help them to focus on their positive attributes

The appearance of body hair can be a cause of great concern. With boys the problem can lie in not having enough; with girls it can be having too much. Hairs on a girl's breasts can make her suicidal unless she is assured that the hairs will disappear (or can be removed with tweezers) and she is forewarned that she will eventually end up with them in the armpits, the base of the pelvis, and on the arms and legs. She also needs to know that whether she has a lot of hair or very little in these places, *it is still perfectly normal.* Occasionally, some women do end up with an excessive amount of hair on the body or face, and in these cases medical advice should be sought as treatment with hormones is possible.

Sadly, the image currently being promoted by the media, the fashion houses and magazines, all suggest to women that only a certain kind of body is acceptable. As most of us can't hope to come anywhere near this 'ideal', we end up feeling inadequate. The people responsible should consider the disastrous outcome of such messages, especially to the most vulnerable: the emerging young adult.

Young men also have image problems. They are not all going to look like Mr Universe, no matter what they do. Some are going to be short, others awkwardly over average height; some will have no hair on their chests, others may feel the need to shave it off.

It is absolutely no good telling your child that the way they look doesn't matter and isn't important – it is to them. The only way to combat the force of such messages is to help your child develop a good sense of self-esteem; there are always going to be areas in which they can do well and feel good about themselves, and you should encourage them to build on these.

WHAT'S SEX, MUM?

This is an area which concerns many parents, and one which must be handled carefully.

If you live in the city, knowledge of sex and reproduction is usually learned by watching TV, reading books specially written for young children, through school, or by talking to friends. If you live in the countryside, on the other hand, your children will have witnessed the natural process of reproduction in the animal world, and their understanding of the subject may come rather more easily.

One Sunday, returning home from church by car, one of my sons asked how children were produced. I explained in simple words, likening it to examples from nature.

'Do hens do it that way?' one asked. 'Yes,' I replied, 'with the help of the cockerel.'

We were passing a farm at the time. 'Oh! Can we stay and watch?' he asked. They had seen the act a hundred times, but now that it was directly linked to human birth they looked at it rather differently.

'And did you and Daddy make us that way?' another child asked.

'Yes,' I assured him. 'With more love and caring than we see in nature, for people are more able to experience such feelings.'

'Is it nice?' another enquired.

'Yes, it is a lovely feeling.'

That seemed to satisfy their curiosity for the time being, but I found myself wondering what I would have done if they had asked, 'Can we watch you and Daddy do it next time?' We had always made our bedroom a private place, only visited on invitation or when the children were ill or frightened by a bad dream, and so I didn't need to worry about the effect on them had they walked in at such a moment.

A mother told me of the occasion when her eight-year-old daughter asked her what sex was, and how people came to have babies. She said she found it very difficult to talk about the subject as it had always been taboo in her family. Aware of her responsibility she did explain it in a simple way so that her daughter could understand. Afterwards the little girl looked at her and said, 'Thank you very much, Mummy, for telling me.' She realized they had shared a very special experience which had drawn them closer together. In a way, she had been saying, *This is life. It is the most wonderful thing on earth. It is beautiful. All creation is a gift.* This is the sort of thing that makes bringing up children so inspiring and worthwhile.

If children are treated with respect from an early age, they quickly learn to respect other people's feelings and their privacy.

A little tap on the door before you go in to read them a bedtime story, or to give them a goodnight kiss, is a perfect way to demonstrate that you understand that they too have a special place to which they can retreat. This need for a space of their own is one of the reasons why so many children build a den; it may only be a few sheets of cardboard, a space in the corner of the room, a certain bush in the garden, but it is theirs, and sacred.

As their bodies begin to change, teenagers become very embarrassed and self-conscious, and feel they are stupid for not knowing certain things, or that you, as a parent, can't possibly understand. Most teenagers do not think of their parents as being sexually active. They want you to be there in the role of parent, but not to be experiencing feelings they think are special to them.

A mixed family helps children to understand physical differences.

Watching the new baby having a diaper changed will encourage questions which you should have no difficulty in answering. Young people also tell me that biology lessons at primary school, before anything much started happening personally, were a great help. Others believe that learning from friends was easiest for them, although there is a danger here that they might learn some half-truths and myths that can cause problems in the future. Access to a medical dictionary can also be very useful; there are many questions that a teenager might not want to ask aloud. Expert opinion in a reference book can be very reassuring.

Teenagers experience great fears about changes, such as how long a penis should be, and at what angle it is supposed to point when an erection takes place; and does a lump in the breast or an overlarge nipple mean you are turning into a woman, or is it cancer?

Learning about sex is exciting to a boy and pretty soon he is going to start to wonder if he can *do it* ... Boys are initially only interested in their genital organs and how they perform; they start maturing sexually at around thirteen years of age. The erections they will have been experiencing are often associated with some exciting stimulus – even sitting an exam can cause a very inconvenient erection. And then there is the worry, *Will anyone notice the bulge in my trousers?* They begin to have wet dreams, start to masturbate, and to talk with their pals in the hope of gaining reassurance or additional knowledge. Here again, a comprehensive factual book will help. Boys shouldn't be made to feel that exploring their bodies and experimenting is wicked or depraved, but must understand that it should not become obsessive behaviour.

Despite all the myths surrounding masturbation (in boys and girls) there is no evidence that it is physically harmful. It can be helpful in that it releases sexual tension and helps the young emerging adult to understand his or her body, its likes and dislikes, before becoming sexually active with a partner.

Evidence shows that boys who are really keen on sport and direct their energies into physical activities are more likely to have a balanced attitude towards sex and are less likely to become involved in intense early relationships.

To start with, girls are almost always more concerned with romantic feelings than sexual involvement; they get crushes on teachers, sometimes on older girls, pop stars, or distant members of their own family. Girls do need to be told that boys become sexually aroused very easily (they still have to learn to control their responses). Although girls may not set out to be provocative in their dress or behaviour, it is often interpreted in this way by the male. Teenage girls soon recognize that they have tremendous power through their bodies, but don't understand that at first boys are much more interested in the mechanics of sex than in romance. His motorbike may, during adolescence, be as important to a boy as his girlfriend; this, however, is something a girl will find almost impossible to understand. One reason girls often find older males attractive is that they have learned how to prioritize their interests and respond in ways that make the girl feel good about herself.

Note: There are many other aspects of sexuality that are going to concern teenagers as they mature, such as disease, contraception, homosexuality and impotence, and these will be discussed later.

HOW DO I LOOK?

Although your teenager desperately wants to have your confirmation that he looks okay, he will still need the approval of his contemporaries. His clothes, hair style – even the language he uses – has to fit in with his chosen group. Teenagers will vehemently defend the appearance of friends as well as themselves, and tell you it is wrong to judge people by the way they look, but they are, at the same time, most anxious about their own appearance. Expressing your disapproval is negative at best, and causes outright conflict at worst. This part of his life is his, and unless there is a potential health hazard (for example, if he is refusing to wash) it is well to let it take its course. If his change in clothing, hair style and speech does no actual harm, it is far better to let him work through this stage and eventually decide how *he* wants to present himself to the world.

Where your opinion and expertise will really count is in the physical body your teenager presents to the world. *Mum, what can I do about these spots . . . or dandruff . . . or rash . . . or bulging waist-line?* This is a cry for help. Don't be tempted to tell him that it doesn't matter, or that he will grow out of it. Right now he needs constructive help and advice.

The skin, due to developing sex hormones, does often have a struggle to get things right. Nothing will miraculously change overnight, and despite all the adverts for various preventive treatments, the best cure does seem to be cleanliness; washing regularly helps to remove oil and bacteria from the skin. Oil glands and the surrounding tissue can become infected thus causing that pussy spot which looks and feels like Mount Vesuvius to your teenager. The temptation to squeeze an offending spot is hard to resist, but this action can cause infection or scarring; leaving it alone is best. Having a preparation prescribed by a doctor can help and, if acne persists, suggest to your teenager that he seeks medical help. Most adults do not suffer from acne, but this offers little consolation to the self-conscious young person. Make-up clogging the pores doesn't help either, so tell your teenager to be sure to remove this with a good soap. I have found that perfume-free soap can help greatly.

For special occasions a cover-up skin make-up can be used by boys as well as girls, but using this all the time will stop the skin from breathing, and also prevents fresh air reaching it. One skin disorder that is much helped by exposure to the sun, in moderation, is psoriasis.

I have had some success in treating skin disorders with hypnotherapy. If your teenager's problem is preventing him from getting on with his life, you may like to consider consulting a qualified hypnotherapist.

A good diet – without becoming fanatical over it – will help with development, shape and general health, but there is little evidence that it actually affects what is happening beneath the skin of the changing adolescent.

Vitamins are essential to good health. They are readily available in all fruits and vegetables and eating them raw between meals is a good way of obtaining the maximum benefit. Even now, I find a bowl of raw carrots left on the kitchen table rapidly disappear; eaten by young and old with equal enthusiasm. As a starter, I sometimes serve slices of apple and cheese which are also appreciated – they don't take much preparation either!

Remember that calories are all about energy. Food contains calories. The more you take in, the more energy needs to be expended to use up those calories. The problem is that many teenagers like to lounge around a lot of the time and exercise is often seen as unattractive. Where you still provide the meals, you can help by ensuring that little fat or oil is used, and by avoiding adding extra sugar to dishes. Talking to my youngest son recently, who lives away from home and does his own cooking, he told me that he no longer eats butter on toast or in sandwiches and that he doesn't use fat or oil to cook. I asked how he managed with stir-fries which I know he loves. 'I use a drop of water', he told me. I've since tried it and it works just as well.

This goes to demonstrate that once your teenager decides to do something about his health and appearance he makes things easy for you. Where rebellion is the rule of the day, you may have to use more subtle means. After all, we took good care of what went into their mouths when they were young, why stop now when it is equally important? This doesn't mean that you never serve up lemon meringue pie or stew and dumplings again – an occasional treat won't destroy all you have achieved. But make it a rule that 'all things in moderation' dominates in the kitchen.

I HATE MY BODY!

This is a cry most parents are going to hear at this stage. The problem most likely to cause heartache in boys is feeling they are too skinny – they don't look macho; with girls it is believing they are overweight. Reassure them, but don't underestimate these fears; they are real. Some children may even become suicidal over their appearance.

Never laugh when young teenagers express their anxieties, and do try to avoid talking about them to others. It is important to cultivate respect and a caring attitude towards the changing child. A good guide is to ask yourself, *Would I say this about my friend?* If you can begin treating your teenager as you would a friend you will avoid many damaging remarks, find it easier to let go, and a new, very satisfying relationship will evolve.

Mothers are often to blame for their children being over-weight. Using food to express love is very natural. *Eat this up, there's a good boy*, is suggesting that if you want to please Mummy and be good, that is what you do. Or if you are told, *I spent all morning preparing this for you*, it becomes impossible to leave it. In a way, your child eating what you have prepared becomes a test of love and a demonstration of gratitude. No matter how much junk food your teenager is eating elsewhere, insist on healthy eating at home. You don't have to cook chips every night because that's all Jimmy likes. If jacket potatoes are disliked there are still pastas, rice and wholemeal bread to help fill a hungry stomach.

If *you* have a poor body image you are likely to pass this belief on to your child. If you are happy with the way you look you set the best example for your teenager to follow.

COMPARISONS

Comparisons are so damaging that we must think about how often we use them, however well-meaning we are trying to be.

Of course they can be helpful, but more often than not they cause feelings of inadequacy and failure. I have spoken to many parents and young people, and one thing that keeps coming up is that every child is different. To be compared with older or younger brothers or sisters can be hurtful and insulting. Remember the tip about treating your child with the same respect you would give a friend? Would you say to a friend, *Why can't you be more like your brother?* or *I think if you had your hair re-styled like your sister's it would look better?*

We need to recognize that our children's behaviour is going to change as they develop, and behaviours seen as acceptable or cute in younger members of the family are no longer appropriate for the older child. It is not cheek or defiance if they point this out; they are trying to communicate what they are honestly feeling. At the same time they may greatly resent privileges they see being given to a younger brother or sister which are now denied to them: getting in bed in the morning with Mum and Dad, receiving pocket money without having to work for it, being let off chores because they are too little to do them. If you fail to appreciate what is happening you are going to be confronted with sulks, moods or anger.

Andrea had this attitude until her mother pointed out some of the advantages of being older. Amongst these was being able to stay up later, watch certain TV programmes denied her younger sister, and having her ears pierced. She was reasonable enough to see that her mother was right, and the complaining stopped.

There is almost always some rivalry in a family and there will always be times when one member is feeling that he is, or has been, unfairly treated, no matter how hard you try.

MOOD CHANGES

Variations in mood are caused both by physiological changes in the body, and/or by changing thought patterns. When a young person is going through puberty he is subject to extreme fluctuations of hormones which make his life more complicated: he is not only having to learn to handle new responsibilities involving physical change in his body, but also other changes in his life, some of which can be quite frightening.

Bodily odour (BO) is a problem for many adolescents and they need to be told carefully and in privacy how to deal with this problem. None of us likes to be told that something about us is offensive, but if we are made aware of it tactfully we ought to be grateful.

As your child becomes aware of her body she is likely to become introspective and spend hours in the bathroom. It may look as if she has become very selfish, but it is natural for her to be absorbed in herself at this time; she has a lot of adjusting to do. She may feel that she is out of control, and a parent yelling accusations only emphasizes how alone she is with her problems.

Things that never seemed to bother your child before will suddenly be blown up out of all proportion. A birthmark no one is ever likely to see suddenly just *has* to be removed, or it will ruin your daughter's whole life. Ears that stick out may well have your son wearing a cap – even indoors – resulting in you thinking he has turned into an ill-mannered lout, despite all your training! In reality he is highly embarrassed by what he sees as an absurd deformity.

A young friend, whom I have known since she was a baby, told me that it wasn't until she had her first boyfriend she realized that she couldn't be the freak she had believed she was. She reasoned that no one would want to go out with her if she really looked as ridiculous as she had imagined.

There are some problems your teenager will need to resolve for herself, but it's nice to know that you are there and will listen, without condemnation, to her thoughts and fears if she chooses to confide in you. If you can possibly avoid it, don't use the word 'silly'. Part of your teenager may know when this applies to her fears, while another part is crying out for reassurance.

Crossed arms, hands constantly kept in pockets, hair hanging over the face, and so on, are often used to cover up what the adolescent sees as abnormalities. As their self-esteem grows and their bodies come once more into a balanced whole, these habits should disappear.

Explaining to your adolescent what is happening, why excess fat has gathered in certain places, why they feel awkward or ungainly, can be reassuring. You may consider suggesting that they talk to their friends about the way they feel; this can result in a tremendous feeling of relief. *Oh! Do you feel like that too? I thought it was only me!* Pre-menstrual tension is an area where, although girls may talk about their periods in a *What a nuisance!* attitude, they omit to mention the emotions they are struggling to control.

Whether your child shares her moods with you or masks them beneath a devil-may-care attitude, they are going to happen. Denial never resolved anything. If she is unusually quiet, a gentle *Want to talk?* may be all that is needed. If she goes into her bedroom and slams the door, leave things for half-an-hour and then pop up with a cup of tea or coffee and ask if she's okay. She will probably say 'yes' regardless of how she is feeling, but you will have shown her that you are there if she needs you, and that you care.

Shouting at your teenager to snap out of a mood, to get her backside off that bed and find something useful to do, will not achieve anything except resentment and hurt feelings. There will be times when bad moods seem to be too prolonged and you do need to intervene, but you can't *make* your child talk to you or 'snap out of it'. If serious depression sets in your child needs to see a professional person. Maybe she is being bullied at school, ostracized, or even pressurized beyond her academic ability by teachers.

Falling in love for the first time can be the most fantastic feeling; it can also be filled with fears, doubt, confusion and despair. Sharing one of your own such experiences with your son or daughter will help them to realize that although you can do nothing about the situation, you do understand.

While visiting a friend the other day I met his son whom I hadn't seen for some years. We spoke about the time when he was seventeen and his mother had died, and he told me how badly he had behaved towards his father. 'I don't know what made me do it. Maybe I just wanted to hurt someone because I was hurting so much,' he told me. This behaviour only stopped when he left home. He looked across at his father with a smile. 'Now we are the best of mates,' he said. 'I don't feel like that at all any more.'

It may be confusing, but sometimes our children really don't know why they are behaving badly and they don't know how to get out of that mode. To them, it may feel as if the whole world is against them and no-one understands how they feel. At times like this distraction will sometimes help. I recall my own mother suggesting that I went out for a long walk when I felt this way. I would climb to the top of a hill, completely out of breath, sit there and look at the scene – or a starlit night – often thinking how awful life was; by the time I returned home I was usually feeling better.

My daughter tells me that when she was struggling with over-load of emotions as a teenager, she would often return home, off-load them onto me, then go out again, meet a friend, and an hour later would be feeling fine again. It wasn't until she matured that she realized she often left me worrying about her all day, believing her to be in the depths of despair when she was actually enjoying herself. Teenage emotions do get caught up on extreme highs and lows, so try not to get swept away by them. They are really ever so normal. It is also a fact that you are going to hear far more about their downs than the good feelings – funny how so often they forget to share those!

Drastic action may need to be taken in order that you don't get dragged into a state of despair yourself. Certainly a child leaving home sounds pretty extreme, especially if he is under age. If temporary suitable accommodation can be found, the teenager will often return in a few weeks (sometimes it takes only days!) with a completely changed outlook. I sometimes think that swopping teenagers with a friend can work very well. It is surprising how much better your child will behave in some-one else's house.

You may be able to work something out with your teenager that sounds attractive to them, or reasonable enough for them to give it a try.

- Let's agree to get on together as best we can until the end of term and then you can go and stay with your grandparents, or go to summer camp, or do the archery course at the college – or whatever you think will appeal.
- A time set aside for the family to come together and talk about their grievances can help to iron out a lot of misunder-standings. Teenagers need to be encouraged to talk about their feelings where they know they will get a fair and sympa-thetic hearing. It may help to ask, 'How can we help you to feel happier about this?' or 'What do you think we can do to help?'
- Sometimes you may have to be really tough, like friends of mine whose son failed to go into college for six weeks and was threatened with being expelled. This meant that they would have to repay the whole of his grant which they simply could not afford. Here they had to say, 'You go to college and finish the course and *then* you can decide about your future. But right now there is no option. You put your feelings and what you want to do on hold until the end of the course.'
- Avoid yelling back and getting upset if you possibly can. This may involve agreeing to disagree. You can let your teenager know you are upset and walk away until you have both calmed down sufficiently to discuss the problem effectively. (It is always better and more productive to deal with only one problem at a time.)

Lucy (who had divorced and remarried) and her new husband had reached a desperate situation with her son, Ian, when the boy's father volunteered to have Ian for the summer holidays. He could help on the farm, he said. After four weeks Ian was so glad to return to his mother's home that his whole behaviour pattern became more considerate and helpful – almost as if he were saying, *Don't send me there again!*

3   *Understanding Emotions*

SHYNESS

Shyness or self-consciousness is a great handicap for many young people. Not always apparent, shyness can be covered up by quite bizarre or unexpected behaviour: your son becomes deeply immersed in his studies, spending hours doing homework in his bedroom; your daughter refuses to eat out; boys clown around a lot, or start dressing in ways that horrify you – like my son's friend with the Mohican haircut – hoping to draw attention away from themselves. The man who speaks loudly at the bar is often still struggling with shyness or feelings of inadequacy. We would do well to pause and ask ourselves *why* someone behaves in this way before pre-judging others.

Why don't you go out? Find something to do? Join a club? can all send the child even deeper into herself. She may have a strong desire to do these things even though she denies this. She simply doesn't know how to break out of the shell she has built around her.

Most of us are shy, or at least reticent, in some areas of our lives, while being well able to cope in others. As a teacher, or accountant, or bank manager, you may have no difficulty in talking to those whom you help through your work, but the thought of standing up in public and making a speech is a terrifying prospect. At school, or college, the chances are that your child will *have* to stand up in front of the class and speak on a subject or lead a debate. Truancy may be the only way out.

Someone I know told me that he never went to school when he was supposed to speak in front of the class, or when there was an examination. 'I just couldn't bear to stand up there making a fool of myself,' he said. I asked him what made him think he would be considered foolish. 'They'd all laugh anyway,' he told me. 'We all did, whenever anyone got up to do a talk.'

Now this is a hard one to crack. Joining in the ridicule or laughter makes you feel safe; being laughed *at* is another matter. You might think, as everyone laughed, it wouldn't be taken seriously, or that the recipient of the joking would not feel upset – but it doesn't work that way.

Some people are more sensitive than others, no matter how hard they try to hide it. The way to combat this is to build up their confidence as early on as possible. Teachers should help in this area, but they often have to cope with large classes, an overload of paperwork, new rules and regulations, changed curriculum and/or may not have studied psychology and do not notice the shy child who is struggling.

Here are some suggestions you may find helpful (if you are already doing all this it's still nice to know you are on the right track):

- Keep communicating – this means also learning to really listen.
- Look for areas in your child's life where you can genuinely offer praise.
- Use encouragement – not bribery.
- Take your child's problems seriously; don't ever tell them that their fears are silly – to them they are very serious.
- Consider their opinions and ideas as you would if they were offered by a friend or colleague – you could learn a lot.
- Welcome their friends into your home – your child may at first feel safer in his/her own environment.
- Support their hobbies and interests – when we are good at something it helps to build self-esteem.

In my work I see many adults who have never learned to cope with the problem of shyness and feelings of self-consciousness.

Some people are born timid; it is part of their personality to be cautious and reserved. As adults they will have developed their own strategies for coping, but those who have experienced some trauma resulting in feelings of self-consciousness usually have not.

Tips to pass on to your teenager:

- Not everyone is looking at you, nor are they necessarily even interested in how you look, what you say, or what you are doing.
- Remember that people are mostly interested in themselves.
- When you are out socially, look for someone who appears shy or on their own and approach them – they will be so relieved to discover someone they can talk to, or at least stand next to.
- If you don't know what to say, ask people about themselves – questions that require a simple 'yes' or 'no' are not helpful in promoting conversation – be really interested.

If you don't already do so, start participating in a sport or competitive activity with your teenager; allow her points or give yourself a handicap if necessary so that you can have a good game together. This will help her confidence enormously. The earlier you start this the better. The day that she beats you fair and square is one you can thoroughly enjoy. After all, *you* helped her to get there.

BULLYING

Bullying is one of the greatest emotional traumas a child has to endure; it should never be brushed aside and neither should the child be told that it is his problem and that he has to learn to deal with it himself. If he were that strong and able, he would not become a victim.

Don't feel that you have failed if you need help to tackle this problem. When children are very young their parents appear all-powerful – they think that we know everything. As they grow older that illusion is going to be broken whatever you do, so it really is all right to admit to your child if you don't know something or how to cope in a certain situation. You then need to assure him that you know of someone (or will find someone) who can help. There are experts now in every area of life, and if your child is intimidated or bullied help is available.

The first thing is to recognize that something bad is going on. There seems to be an unwritten code of behaviour that prevents children revealing the awful truth when they are being bullied or intimidated. Many live in fear of what will happen to them if they speak out. It may seem hard to realize that your child – who never did anything to harm anyone else – has become a victim. The sad truth is that you don't have to *do* anything to be bullied; it can simply be the way you look, or the way the bully interprets the way you look to him. Bullying can take the form of verbal harassment or physical abuse.

If you have a particularly bright child he can also suffer bullying. He may deliberately drop back in class to avoid being put in the limelight by the teacher.

Be alert to changes in your child's behaviour. If you suspect bullying bring the conversation round to the subject, perhaps by recalling an incident when you were bullied as a child. Remember too that some teachers can be bullies. When the problem is happening in school, get down there and talk to someone; they must ensure the safety of the pupils. Do not allow anyone to pass it off, or attempt to make you feel as if you are a neurotic parent. If your child is skiving off school or using any little ache or pain as an excuse not to go, he has a problem. Of course it could be the work, but if this is so he still needs extra help in order to catch up and be able to cope.

I watched in amazement a recent TV show on this subject and heard a school bully say of her victim, 'She looks as if she thinks she's better than us.' This was enough for the gang of bullies to punch her in the face, spit on her, pull her hair, and physically prevent her from going where she wanted. In a case like this the bully is obviously feeling inferior; she is the one with the problem, and hasn't yet learned how to address it.

Retaliation sometimes works and you may decide with your child that he should learn one of the martial arts of self-defence; he can at least then protect himself and this will usually cause others to back off. We all have the right to defend ourselves. But remember that all too often retaliation only prolongs the situation.

A confident responsible adult who can ensure that this practice of bullying does not continue needs to intervene. Many schools now use ground rules to which both bullies and the victims agree: no name calling, no physical bullying, no talking about each other, and agreeing to stay away from each other. Suggesting they become friends rarely works.

One very important step in combating bullying is to help build your child's confidence. You cannot fight every battle for him and eventually he is going to have to learn how to cope without you; confidence is the key. This though, is a gradual process, and your child may need your intervention right now. There is a difference between a bit of teasing and leg-pulling and the systematic demoralization of a person. You should know your child better than anyone else and be able to gauge when it is right to intervene and when to leave him to resolve his own problems.

Bullying can prevent your child from working well at school; it may cause him to try and change his image; it may make him aggressive or angry; it may turn him into a recluse. Whatever the response, you can be sure it is making him very unhappy. In extreme cases, as we know, teenagers have committed suicide as a result of bullying.

If your child feels he can't talk to you and you suspect bullying, ask a close friend of his to talk to him. You may get second-hand information that will help. Alternatively, make use of one of the various organizations that are now available in most towns and cities. These usually work closely with schools, although, sadly, there are still schools who deny they have a problem. A list of organizations that will help is given at the end of this book.

Sometimes confronting the bully or making the parents aware will resolve the problem, but this needs to be undertaken with great sensitivity; most parents are not too willing to accept that their child is a bully.

Awful though it may sound, some of our children are the bullies. This is a very serious problem, not just because of the harm it causes to others, but also because of what it is doing to them. If you suspect your child may be a bully, try to find out why and deal with the problem. If you can't, seek help. Again, don't hesitate to use the school or an appropriate organization. Bullying is often the result of a poor self-image or a hidden response to fear; it can be a behaviour observed in the way parents deal with life. If you tend to be belligerent or you frequently put down other people or ridicule them, you are setting a very poor example for your child.

FEARS – REAL OR IMAGINED?

Can you remember anything that used to worry or frighten you as a youngster? A teacher perhaps? Thinking you had cancer? That you were sexually abnormal? That no one would like you because your nose was too big? Were you scared of the dark, people who were drunk, spiders, dogs, water? The list is endless, for we are all capable of being afraid of anything. I have dealt with several cases of people who are afraid of buttons! This may seem absolutely ridiculous, but it usually stems from having choked on a button as a baby, or having had buttons on an adult's jumper scraped against the face. It is very important to try to identify the root of the fear – if it comes from a past experience, use Exercise 1 (p. 12) to help you. If it is a very deep-rooted fear, consult a counsellor or therapist.

One of the more real fears for the adolescent is that of not being liked. The only way to deal with this is for them to build friendships; for some, one or two friends is sufficient, others need a whole crowd. If school life doesn't seem to offer this they are going to feel different and rejected. There are outside school activities that can offer real opportunities to share and communicate. Some teenagers find it easier to befriend someone who needs them: they may choose to help in an animal sanctuary, join a first-aid group such as the Red Cross, or help with blind or physically disabled children.

When teenagers say they have nothing to do, they are usually saying that there is nothing they *want* to do at the moment. They need to have space and time to daydream; fantasizing is part of growing-up, and it is not wasted time unless it is either used as an escape from the real world or gets in the way of school work and progress.

Our imaginations do rule our world. When we picture something in a negative way we are going to find it hard to follow it through; when we see a positive outcome we are encouraged to proceed. If your teenager is seeing too many things from a negative point of view, helping her to replace these pictures with ones that make her feel good will give her the confidence to move on. When she says something like, *I can't see me doing that!*, this is exactly what she means – she really cannot *see* it happening. Practising something inside your head and seeing a positive outcome makes a profound difference.

We also condition our beliefs by making statements concerning things that haven't even happened: *Everyone will think I'm a fool! No one will like me – or speak to me. I won't be able to do it. I'm useless at everything.*

A gentle reminder of some of their successes is useful – even if they do brush them aside as being 'nothing', your words will have an effect. Try using examples that go back a long way, the unconscious mind will take your words on board and make constructive use of them: 'Do you remember how many times you tried to swim before you were able to?' or 'Do you know that Einstein failed in arithmetic at school and Edison was expelled at the age of thirteen, and see what they achieved?' It is what we learn from our experiences that is useful and equips us best to cope with life. Sharing your experiences rather than your opinions is a far better way to communicate.

When a person keeps telling you they are useless and will never succeed at something, they are often needing you to contradict them and assure them that they are able and they will succeed. Confident people do not have the same need to evaluate themselves by the way others perceive them.

Some young people's expectations of themselves can be unrealistically high. Nothing is achieved without effort, either physical and/or mental, and being persistent is something they have to learn. When my own grandchildren tell me they are no good at doing something, having expected to get it right first time and failed, I remind them of how often they fell off their bicycles before they learned to ride.

It will be helpful to share some of your own fears with your teenager, especially where they involve the family. Although you don't want to burden them with your problems, you enable them to feel grown-up by letting them into your world. You may also be surprised at their response.

Real fears affecting your teenager may include being forced to take drugs or alcohol, abuse, rape, and cruel treatment by certain teachers. Phobias also result in real fear: the dark, being afraid to go to the dentist or hospital, having an injection, eating certain foods, going out of doors, getting into a lift. Any of these can affect the well-being of the phobic, or strictly limit her activities, and need to be resolved.

Note: How to deal with phobias is dealt with in my book *Are You In Control?* (see Recommended Reading).

ANGER

Anger is a very powerful emotion and it can be entirely destructive. It is almost impossible to communicate logically when we are very angry. The only thing anger reveals is that we are very upset about something.

Anger can be a release of energy and happens frequently with younger people because they haven't yet learned control. Where anger flares up suddenly and dies away almost as quickly there is no need to get concerned; this stage will soon pass. If, however, the feelings of resentment behind the anger are not dealt with, they will continue to present themselves at the least provocation.

Anna's teenage son came in one day and immediately began to get angry with her over everything; the dinner wasn't ready and he had to go out; his football kit hadn't been washed, and so on. She knew she hadn't done anything to warrant this outburst so finally asked, 'Why are you so angry with me?' He looked at her in surprise and then said, 'Sorry, it's really nothing to do with you. I've had a horrendous day at college.'

Sometimes, when our children can't release feelings outside the home, they use (subconsciously) the one person they believe will forgive them – no matter what. Knowing this, we can make some allowances; understanding means you don't have to react or retaliate, or take it personally – it is the beginning of communication. Asking, 'Can we find a better way of dealing with this?' will help direct the energies into a more satisfactory outcome. Your teenager may then see that his emotions are not producing a positive outcome and that by talking, or letting go, or even trying to understand from another point of view, he achieves something more positive than just 'blowing his top'. Using 'road rage' as an example, you may be able to demonstrate how sometimes, no matter how badly the other person behaves, you simply have to let it go.

Where anger is a response to a frustrating situation, help your child to seek alternative ways of dealing with the problem which are more productive. When one consciously decides to do nothing, or to let a situation go, you have not given in but have made a choice. This way you still remain in control.

JEALOUSY

This emotion is a very unhappy one. Often it is caused when a second child arrives and the older one no longer has the 100 per cent attention she has grown to believe is her right, and this resentment can carry on into the teenage years and beyond. Although there may be some compensation in being older, the child will focus entirely on the negatives. Things may get out of all proportion in her mind until it feels as if everyone else is better off than she is, has more, and is more loved. Most parents try to be fair, and although you struggle to point this out, your child may refuse to look at anything other than from her own negative point of view.

Often, unwittingly, relatives or outsiders can cause many negative feelings. I have a sister who is one year older than me, and when we were children, people would ask why I didn't have curly hair like my sister; others would tell her that I was catching her up and would soon be taller – as if that were a bad thing. We went through stages of actively hating each other and it was only as we matured and developed our individuality that we no longer felt we had to compete. Many adults still have feelings of sibling rivalry that have never been resolved.

By being as fair as you can, offering your child assurance, and steering her towards things in which she can excel or use her own unique talents, you can help her to overcome jealousy.

ENVY

Although envy is often closely linked to jealousy, it is different. It is a powerful longing to possess things or attributes we see that other people have and that we do not. This ought to spur us on, but if we lack the commitment to pursue similar goals, we can end up feeling bitter and resentful and discontent with almost every aspect of our life.

If your teenager seems unduly concerned over what someone else has, help her to define specifically what this is. If it proves to be a good quality, she can set goals to achieve something similar. If it is materialistic, help her to recognize whether it is the possession she envies, or what it represents – admiration, social standing, independence. Having done this, discuss how she can work towards this goal if she really believes it will benefit her or make her happy.

Because adolescence is a time of frequent change in direction, she may well lose interest in something and move off on another tack. This doesn't necessarily demonstrate that she has no staying power but that this thing is no longer important to her. Where it appears to be a more serious problem you may need to discuss this and offer the support or advice needed.

Your child may at times appear like an alien to you

STRESS

Many parents are astonished to discover that their children are suffering from stress and depression. What on earth have they got to be depressed about? A lot, in fact. They listen to the news, read papers, watch TV and it seems like they have no future. After years and years of education, where are they going to get a job? And what about all the things the media tell you that you can now die from before you even reach twenty?

The problem is that the media rarely presents good news; the more we know of others, the more we hear of death, rape, disaster, war and other atrocities. It is no good telling your teenager, who may have just started taking an interest outside her immediate world, that it was worse in your day. It is *now* that matters to her.

Watch out for the child who carries the load; she is usually the peace-maker, often making herself responsible for brothers and sisters. She will be very close to her mother and will try to take on responsibilities to make life easier for Mum. When she can't, she may become very depressed.

More and more families are splitting up and many teenagers may also have to cope with their parents' depression, sense of failure and frustration. It would be unlikely that every aspect of your life is perfect, but your child really would like it to be so; that would give him the assurance he is seeking. This isn't the time to say, *I'm miserable . . . fed up . . . likely to lose my job.*

Be realistic, and try to help your teenager deal with problems constructively. Many things that cause depression are due to the way we view something. By turning a problem into a challenge it is easier to cope with it and to find a solution.

Many reasons for depression come from a poor self-image. Teenagers most often value themselves through other people's eyes: *If no one wants to employ me . . . or be my friend . . . or go out with me . . . there must be something wrong with me.* Their behaviour may be sending out negative messages, and if so this needs to be addressed. Again, lack of confidence causes them to protect themselves by creating barriers and they are not even aware that they are doing so. If you think your teenager has this problem, perhaps you could get her to use the following exercise:

Exercise 2 – Dealing with stress

1 Take ten minutes off from doing anything else and relax, either on your bed or in an armchair. Close your eyes and breathe deeply for a few minutes. Concentrate on the feelings you experience as you physically let go and relax. Start with your toes and feet . . . now your leg muscles . . . your stomach muscles . . . your chest . . . Notice how the rhythm of your breathing slows down as you relax . . . Now let all of those tiny muscles in your head relax. Allow a calm peaceful expression to spread across your face. Feel your jaw relax . . . Imagine all the stress and tension in your head, your neck, your shoulders, flowing away down through your arms and out through the tips of your fingers . . .

2 Be still for a few minutes and breathe deeply.

3 Now imagine walking on a beautiful beach. It is evening time and there is no one else around. Smell the sea, feel the gentle breeze on your face.

4 You stop at the water's edge and watch the waves. The tide is going out.

5 You begin thinking about those things that make you anxious and stressed. As you name them to yourself give them a shape (you could see anger represented as a red ball; despair a black cloud; rejection an old jigsaw puzzle). Now throw them out into the water, one by one. The waves plunge over them, drawing them down and away into the middle of the ocean where they are lost forever.

6 When you have completed this, turn and walk up across the beach feeling relaxed and peaceful. You are feeling strong and positive, ready to return to your world, knowing that if ever

you become stressed again you only have to picture being on this beach and throw out any negative feelings that are bothering you into the water.

I have asked a great many teenagers, and young people in their twenties, about the worst and best things about being a teenager; here are my findings:

Worst
- Being treated like a child
- Not being taken seriously
- Parents' break-up and divorce
- Parent dying
- People's expectations of them being too high
- Being rejected by boyfriend/girlfriend
- Shyness and self-consciousness
- Frustration due to limitations set by age
- Too much responsibility
- Being bullied
- Moving house and changing schools
- Older siblings teasing and bullying
- Not being allowed the freedom of older brothers and sisters
- Prolonged illness in the family

Of all these, 'Being treated like a child' was the most frequent 'worst thing'.

Best
- Feeling that you are capable of anything – that you will live forever
- Freedom to make your own choices
- Freedom to experience new things
- Discovering what you are capable of
- Leaving home and being able to do what you want
- Friends and social life
- Sport

- Having a horse (or dog) – this can be as good as a friend at
  the time

Here, freedom to experience was most appreciated.

Teenagers do often set themselves impossible goals that cause stress. School and college can also be responsible for overload and pressure that leads to stress.

Being miserable and depressed is quite normal as hormones flood the body and the adolescent learns to cope with new responses and emotions. So long as these feelings are not prolonged they will gradually be replaced by more positive behaviour; when this doesn't happen they may lead to depression and even suicide. Do try to stay tuned in to your teenager.

4   Education

Research has shown that when adults are asked to name the thing they most regret about their teens, it is almost always not having made the most of the educational opportunities available to them. This is borne out by the vast number of people who follow adult education classes, or return to college or take a degree in later life. Almost too late, some discover the value of learning and the satisfaction and opportunities it affords. Try telling this to a bored, rebellious teenager who just can't leave school fast enough!

Not every child is going to be academic, and forcing a reluctant teenager to stay on at school rarely achieves anything positive. Up to a certain age they are required by law to attend school; if they hate it they will be counting the days to leaving. You may be able to insist that they continue until they are eighteen, but you cannot *make* them learn. Forcing them to stay at school or to go on to college creates tremendous resentment and anger. Added to this they may see continued education as forcing them to remain children, when everything inside them is screaming to be free.

You may recall how well you learned in those classes where you had a good teacher whom you liked, or where you were able to study a subject that really interested you. Unfortunately, we still have to cover subjects that, at the time, seem useless or totally boring. People may tell you that all learning helps to train the brain so that it can apply those processes to other subjects, but it is hard to see that far ahead without any first-hand experience. Did you hate geography at school only to find yourself now searching maps of unknown places you wish to visit? Did you think history was dead rubbish until you began to take your vacations in other countries? Did you find English a bore until you needed to write business letters or job applications? When we really want or need to have that knowledge we actively pursue it. I never thought my son would be any good at languages until he fell in love with a French-speaking girl – now *that* worked like magic!

Encouragement can be manipulative – you may be trying to force your ideas on your child without recognizing what you are doing. Pause a moment and ask yourself: 'Do I really want my son to go to university because I never did?'

If your teenager is unhappy in school he will not want to stay there a moment longer than he has to. Things that make a child unhappy include bullying, not being able to cope with certain lessons, humiliation caused by a teacher, feeling self-conscious, hating the environment, longing to be somewhere else. Sometimes study feels like it is just too hard, and the teenager needs a lot of encouragement and support to continue.

Teachers who intimidate or use verbal abuse cause untold misery. A youth came to see me some years ago who suffered from a terrible stammer, which had started when he was five. A tray of paints had been accidentally knocked off a table in class and he had been unjustly blamed. The teacher had made him stay in after school to clear it up. When he ran out of paper towel she made him take off his jumper and use that. He still went in fear of anyone in authority and the hesitation, which had become a stammer, was the result of not being believed when he had spoken the truth; he was scared that anything he said would not be believed. The astonishing part of this story is that the teacher is still employed at that school.

There are many examples of people who have paved their own way and been tremendously successful without attaining a university degree. Also, in many countries where less and less jobs are available, young people may well have a point in questioning the wisdom in staying on at school or going on to university. However, leaving school with no plans or intention of getting employment is not a good alternative. If your son or daughter wants to leave school they must have plans to earn a living and to be able to survive eventually without your support.

It is okay to give constructive advice, but one must also be ready to listen to how the adolescent feels about his present position and future. Most teenagers cannot see beyond the next year, and often a teacher, or adult from outside the family whom your teenager respects, can have more influence at this stage. If you are aware of this you might suggest they discuss their future with this person whose wisdom you also respect. Don't get upset if your child chooses to confide in another adult; this doesn't mean they are rejecting you.

My youngest son says that what helped him decide his future was discussing it with a friend. Together they decided what they both wanted to do with their lives and how they could achieve their goals. He tells me he was grateful that we never interfered but allowed him to make up his own mind.

Some teenagers will want to take time out to see something of the world before they settle down to further education or a job. This is not a bad thing and will help to build independence and mould their character. Finding that they can't cope will probably send some scurrying home – avoid the temptation to say, *I told you so*. At least they had a go.

BE AWARE OF YOUR INTENTIONS

I listened to a friend of mine telling his seventeen-year-old son that if he were in his shoes he would look to change his job and better himself. 'But Dad! I love my job,' he protested. 'It'll never get you anywhere,' his father scorned. 'But I don't want to go anywhere, I'm doing what I want right now.' Whether he thought that his father was asking him to fulfil his own dreams, or whether he believed that his father was afraid he would become a financial burden to him, I don't know. I am certain that when he falls in love and wants to marry and have a home of his own, *then* he will actively look at changing his job or seeking promotion if this is necessary.

Many parents, in driving their children to take advantage of the opportunities they never had, or failed to use, often attempt to get their children to fulfil personal desires. Knowing your child, do you really believe staying at school or going on to university *is* best for him?

A lady approached me some years ago somewhat distressed to discover her son had been hiding his exam results from college and lying to her. She had always believed she had a good relationship with him and felt betrayed by this behaviour. I promised to talk to him. He told me that the business studies course was not what he wanted and he found the pressures were making him very unhappy. At the same time he loved his mother and didn't want to disappoint her.

After discussing with him the things he did like and was good at, he decided that he really wanted to be a chef. He was able to get an apprenticeship and qualified with a first-class chain of restaurants. He then moved abroad where the head chef was French, and so he learned a second language. He now works in a top hotel in Germany and speaks fluent German. Not bad for a boy who thought he was a failure! What's more, he is extremely happy and independent.

Every child is different, even within the same family, and to acknowledge this is important. Because an older brother did well in banking, or a sister went on to succeed at a college of music, this doesn't mean a younger one can, or wishes, to follow the same path.

Do *listen* to your child; it is doing what *he* wants with his life that will dictate his success.

SINGLE-SEX SCHOOLS

You may not have to make this decision, but if you do, is there any real evidence that by segregating the sexes more is achieved? Some will advocate that distraction is avoided and that teenagers do learn better when they are not having to compete with others for the attentions of a certain boy or girl. Boys can behave outrageously in front of girls – this is often to cover embarrassment. Sometimes it is the only way they know to draw attention to themselves.

However, recent research in the UK has shown that most of the single-sex schools are fee-paying and have smaller classes. Also, pupils who attend these schools come from professional families where a better home environment encourages them to work. There wasn't a lot of evidence that separating the sexes resulted in greater academic achievement.

I found that attending a mixed school was invaluable experience. I was one of three daughters and this was my only real opportunity to mix with boys naturally. We had an extremely good relationship with most of the boys at school and would back each other up, offering comfort and support when it was needed. Somehow a boy understanding a situation and telling you to, *Cheer up, you'll soon feel better*, gave more power to the words than if a girlfriend had said them.

Doing gym and swimming together also took away a lot of the mystique; we didn't go around wondering for hours what a boy looked like or how he would behave – we knew. Linda, a sixteen-year-old girl who used to come to help me with my children when they were small, attended a convent school for girls. She told me that she couldn't even imagine eating in front of a boy. To her they seemed like gods from another planet.

You will, no doubt, consider very carefully the advantages and disadvantages when selecting a school for your child.

MOVING SCHOOLS

Moving to a new school is, for almost all children, a traumatic experience. This can result in a sudden lack of confidence and the inability to learn. If you can imagine how you would feel if every so often you were swept away into a totally different environment and had to make new friends and work with people you didn't know, then you will get somewhere near understanding how awful it feels for a child. If they have been taught under another system and know more than the other children they may feel embarrassed or experience victimization; if they seem to know less then they will feel inadequate and stupid.

Where some of their friends move with them it isn't such a problem. But if your job causes you to move location, or you decide to put your child in a different school to that of his friends, expect him to be unhappy, at least at first. Sometimes it can't be helped, or you really believe that separating your daughter from that no-good Cathy is advisable. When you do this, try to stay close and be prepared to spend more time with her at first. After a few weeks she should be holding her own.

An educational inspector recently made me aware of just how traumatic it is for a child to leave the security of junior school at eleven – as they do in many schools – and to find themselves once more the least important amongst an enormous mass of children, some of whom may be eighteen years of age.

The transition from one school to the next can differ considerably. Some children are fortunate and do this in small steps. Those schools that accept children from primary school at nine and teach them until they are thirteen do apparently have a greater chance of giving the child confidence and stability. Unfortunately, lack of funds makes it impossible to alter most education procedures.

Choosing a private school may seem like a good idea, especially if your child has certain talents. There are schools that are very strong on sport, or music, or the sciences. However, if your child goes to a different school to the local children, he is likely to become lonely, ignored, or even bullied. Do go with your child and look at the prospective school. First impressions and that good old 'gut feeling' will be as good an indicator as any brochure.

When one of my sons reached the age of sixteen, we offered him the choice of staying in the private school where he had earned a scholarship (this meant we didn't have to pay a lot towards his education) or moving to a state sixth-form college to do his final two years before moving away to university. He visited the new college twice before deciding to make the change. This meant leaving behind many friends and having to make new ones. For him it worked, and he now looks back on this period as being one of the best in his life. He had to do a lot more work without supervision and to mix with a greater variety of teenagers from all walks of life. He now tells me that this alone proved to be invaluable experience.

Not all education is about passing exams and getting a good job. Learning how to live with people and how to mix socially is also part of education. Several adults I know, who appeared to waste time at college and never obtained formal qualifications, still maintain that this period in their life enabled them to finish growing up. It gave them time to learn how to cope with the outside world in easy stages. They believe they would not have done so well had they gone straight from school into a job.

CONFLICT

When children try to please and really make a noticeable effort in school, it may delight the teacher but can result in misery outside the classroom. Being teacher's pet does nothing for the child in the eyes of his classmates. Another conflict the child has to resolve is that of pleasing the parents and fitting in with his peers. If this seems like an exaggeration, ask yourself how you feel in the company of people who seem socially or intellectually superior – or inferior? You have to be very sure of yourself not to feel at least uncomfortable.

Teenagers have to learn to handle so many conflicting things, and peace and harmony at home will be of invaluable help. Where you do feel you have to put on the pressure, ensure that it is constructive and not destructive. Telling your son that he is stupid, thick or useless, will definitely not have a positive effect.

Being cheeky or downright rude may create the impression that the young person doesn't care about anyone's feelings except his own. Often what they are trying to do is convince themselves that they are 'grown-up' and can make their own decisions. They desperately need to be seen as separate individuals. Showing off in front of their peers reflects the need to impress or to appear important. They have still to discover that needing the approval of others in order to feel good never allows them to develop a true sense of self-worth.

There will be a great difference in your teenager's life when he begins to move in circles outside the home. He will be struggling to adjust to a new body, new ideas, and new responsibilities that are bound to cause confusion. If his only way of releasing tension is at home, understanding will help to avoid conflict. This is a time when it can be very difficult for him to focus on school work and may seem utterly pointless to him anyway. A big hug, for sons as well as daughters, can often give comfort or reassurance in a way that words cannot.

Some teenagers will deliberately promote conflict, testing out their strength and new-found independence. You can either react or refuse to be drawn into pointless battles. Conflict and confrontation allows the teenager to express his feelings, but it is communication that enables a solution to be found.

Homework

Homework is one of the areas of greatest conflict. The way you recall how diligently you studied and how it paid off for you, or

He may be able to work well with headphones acting like an umbilical cord to his hi-fi system

how you regret not having worked harder, will not affect your teenager one iota.

By insisting that there is no noise while your teenager is doing his homework, or that it must be carried out in silence in the bedroom (while the rest of the family watches a favourite TV programme downstairs!) can create resentment. Some children *can* work in a noisy environment – with open-plan offices now used in most big businesses, that ability could be a definite advantage. Your teenager may find he works well with head-phones acting like an umbilical cord to his hi-fi system, so don't nag him into studying in silence. A quiet place to think and work seems logical, and certainly a younger brother screaming or running around will be an irritant, but his own kind of noise can

act as a comforter. (*Note:* Do try to discourage the use of head-
phones over prolonged periods; loud continuous noise will cause
hearing problems in later life.)

If they do not get their homework done, it is far better to
leave the teacher to deal with the problem. Teenagers are going
to have to learn self-discipline and this is a good place for them
to start. Nagging only creates more resentment and rebellion
and rarely achieves long-term positive results.

Don't get involved in helping with your children's homework
or projects unless asked to do so. It really won't help if you do
the work for them, and breathing down their necks while they
struggle to do things the way they have been taught is counter-
productive. The best way to help, if asked, is to be able to point
them in the right direction to find the information.

MOTIVATION

Leaving things until the last minute isn't something only teenagers do. There are plenty of adults who go right through life in
this way. Generally, we put off doing things because we don't do
them well or dislike doing them.

To help teenagers overcome this problem suggest they try
this: Think of something you put off doing that has to be done.
Notice where you place the picture of this inside your head. (It
is generally off to the left or right.) Now move that picture
around and notice how your feelings towards it change when
you bring that image right in front of you. This makes it feel
more immediate and you are prompted to get on with the job.

Six weeks to an exam may feel like an eternity to a teenager.
You know how quickly time passes – they have yet to learn this.
Keeping the picture right in front of them when they think
about something that has to be accomplished really will help
motivation. They can use this same visualization for training in
sport, and, of course, to promote study for exams.

When the thing to be accomplished is seen as a chore, focusing on having completed it can be used as the motivator.

EXAM NERVES

People can really only learn from their own experiences; no one, but no one, can learn from what someone else experiences. They may use tips or act upon advice given but that is different to first-hand experience, and if they do mess things up, it is not your fault. One very important part of growing up is learning to take responsibility for one's actions. The fact that if you neglect your work you get the results you deserve is something young people may have to learn first-hand.

People handle exams differently. Some swot right up until the last minute; others decide to have a complete break the day before so that their minds are fresh. One thing that will help is entering that examination room feeling calm and in control. See if you can get your teenager to do this exercise:

Exercise 3 – Help with exams

1 For a few nights before the exam (or other event that is important to you), lie down on your bed and take a few deep breaths before going to sleep. Focus your eyes on something in front of you and start counting silently backwards from 300. (This helps to quiet the mind and to let go of worries by concentrating on something else.) When your eyes become tired let them close and stop counting.

2 Concentrate on the feelings you experience as you physically let go and relax. Start with your toes and feet ... now your leg muscles ... your stomach muscles ... your chest ... Notice how the rhythm of your breathing slows down as you relax ... Now let all of those tiny muscles in your head relax. Allow a calm peaceful expression to spread across your face. Feel your

jaw relax ... Imagine all the stress and tension in your head, your neck, your shoulders, flowing away down through your arms and out through the tips of your fingers ...

3 Now picture yourself in a quiet peaceful place. Take a few minutes to create the scene. Add sounds, smells and the feel of things, if appropriate.

4 Say quietly to yourself something like this: *When I enter the examination room I will feel mentally alert, calm and in control. I will be able to recall all that I have learned.*

5 Give yourself a code word that you can use if you feel yourself getting tense or anxious during the exam. This can be related to the scene you created.

6 Now picture yourself sitting the exam and say that code word quietly to yourself and repeat your positive affirmation: *I will be able to recall all that I have learned.*

7 You are now ready to drift into your natural state of sleep and you will wake up at the proper time feeling calm and mentally alert.

Where you get a totally negative response to the idea of using this exercise accompanied by a nonchalant *I couldn't care less* attitude, know that at least you tried; your teenager may still use the technique but is not going to admit it to you.

LEARNING DIFFICULTIES

It is not the end of the world if your child has learning problems; special tuition is available at all schools. Very serious problems will probably be dealt with by sending the child to a specialist school. This also applies to very gifted children.

It is important to let an exceptionally bright child lead an average life. Being advanced academically does not mean he is any different to other children; he still needs recreation, to mix socially, and to be foolish at times. Some clever children miss out on all the normal steps of growth.

In England there is now a big movement towards integrating

physically disabled children into ordinary school life. I have seen the results of this and it is very promising. The fit children learn to be caring without smothering, and the disabled child is delighted to be treated as 'normal'.

At one school I visited, the teacher who supervises children with special needs told me this lovely little story. She was standing beside a wheelchair when a visitor to the school asked how old the boy in the chair was. Before she could reply, a girl nearby who heard this piped up saying, 'Why don't you ask him?' A lesson from which we can all learn.

SETTING AN EXAMPLE

Where parents spend each night at the club or down at the pub this is what the child expects to do when he is grown-up. Parents who enjoy learning set an excellent example for their children to follow. This doesn't mean that you have to start going to classes; if you enjoy reading about gardening, photography or psychology, or if you service your own car and enjoy technical magazines relating to practical things you do, your behaviour is telling your child, *This is fun.*

If you never pick up a book, watch informative programmes on TV or debate things of interest, then you are not encouraging your child to have an enquiring mind. Evidence shows that where children come from an environment in which their parents read a lot they develop reading abilities much earlier. If a child comes from a family who are very musical they are much more likely to be interested in music.

WHERE DO YOU GO NEXT?

Many parents and their teenage children have university as their goal. Before exam results are known the teenager may have visited several universities and been offered a place at one or more, dependent on exam results. Some teenagers want the experience of attending university without having any long-term goals. The problem with this is that there may not be many jobs in their chosen field when they finish the course, and this can be very disheartening. Looking realistically at the future is very important at this stage. By eighteen they should have a good idea of how they want to earn a living.

If your son has failed to get a place at university it is still possible to take a degree without attending one. If he has not acquired the examination levels required, there is a 'clearing system' that helps match students with courses. Your careers office will be able to help. The student will have to be prepared to make a lot of phone calls, show enthusiasm, explain why he wants to get on that course and cite any interests or experience in that specific area. One boy made it by explaining that his father was an engineer and owned his own business and that he had grown up in this environment. He got his chance and earned a degree.

As an alternative, further education can be obtained by attending specialist colleges, local technical colleges, private classes or through distance learning courses. Where financial limitations are preventing your teenager moving on to further education there are many areas where you may look for help: in some areas of industry there are employers who may help cover the costs; there are also Further Education Funding Councils, Training and Enterprise Councils, Student Awards. Titles of organizations may differ slightly, but if you look around you may get assistance that can make all the difference.

5   Friends and Influences

Who do you think has the greatest influence on your teenager at the moment? You may think it is her teacher, a particular friend, the gang she hangs out with, an older brother or sister. You may be right, but look beneath the surface and you will realize that the groundwork you have been putting in for the last dozen or more years is the foundation on which future behaviour will be built.

This can mean your child becoming much like you, or it can mean total rejection of all you have taught, but it will still be the most influential force, for better or worse. Knowing this does make one aware of the tremendous responsibility we take on in rearing children. I watch my baby grandson of 10 months and see that already he copies his mother's smile, he holds his head in the same enquiring manner, and his laughter is a good imitation of his father's. Assimilation and copying starts before your child begins to communicate verbally.

You are going to have to sit back and perhaps watch your child go through all kinds of relationships with various people, some of whom you will strongly disapprove. There will be teachers at school who will have an enormous influence, especially when your teenage daughter develops a crush on one. I remember doing this once and had my hair styled to look exactly like Miss Evans'. It was only when everyone laughed and I checked in the mirror that I discovered how weird I looked, and I dropped my imitation and adoring attitude.

MAKING CHOICES

Helping your children make choices when they are still young builds their confidence. You might begin by letting them choose their own clothes, decide what they want to eat in a restaurant, say where they would like to spend the day for a change. Of course they will make mistakes; that is part of the process of learning. Where your teenager keeps changing her mind you will need to be tactful and to handle her indecisiveness delicately.

If this seems as if everything is focused on making the child feel good, remember your power. You do have great influence; you are moulding the future generation that is going to be working and supporting you one day. Having the confidence to make right choices is one of the most important assets we can give to our children. It will help them to withstand peer pressure and to feel safe in following their own intuition.

FEAR

Fear is frequently what makes us try so hard to discourage our children from what we believe are dubious friendships. We are so afraid that if their friends come from a different background, have parents who get into trouble with the police, stay out drinking until all hours, that this is going to be the way our child will end up.

Until proven wrong, credit your teenager with the ability to befriend someone without getting into trouble. She may feel sorry for this person, love their free attitude, or is just curious to see things that would never happen at home. It doesn't mean she is going to become like that.

Gone are the days when you decided with whom they played and who came to stay for a weekend. You can still have some influence, though, by suggesting something along these lines: 'I really liked that girl you brought home last week', or, 'Why don't you bring Jane home one evening? I'll do that new dish you like.' When they do bring friends home, don't embarrass them by being too effusive or giving them the third degree. Be interested, let them chat a little if they feel inclined, and then leave them to it.

Having a separate room where your children can entertain their friends is a great help. If you do not have that kind of space and your son or daughter drags their friend of the opposite sex up into the bedroom and firmly closes the door, you may be forgiven for wondering what is going on. Teenagers rarely get involved in sex if there are other people in the house. In any case, they can simply walk out of the house and find a quiet place somewhere away from your listening ears. You can't prevent this sort of thing from happening, but it does not happen *all the time* as some people would have us believe.

I do think it is unwise to have locks on bedroom doors for safety reasons: fires do happen, and being unable to get to someone who is overcome by fumes and trapped behind a locked door is terrifying. Agreeing to knock before entering should still afford that privacy we all need. It is also a deterrent to experimentation in early teenage. They are going to need a lot of nerve to try anything on, knowing they are not shielded by a locked door.

Learning to stand back and watch your emerging young adult deal with friendships, breaking up, making mistakes, is all part of the letting go process and allowing them to be themselves.

Some peer pressure can be destructive – even dangerous – and needs to be recognized. Where you see signs that your teenager's friends are causing detrimental changes to her behaviour and attitude, wait for the right opportunity and try to discuss your fears with her. Young people are very loyal to their friends and she may defend them despite all that you say, but you will have made an important point and she will know that you are aware.

Up to about the age of thirteen you can usually instigate, if necessary, action that keeps your child apart from certain friends in her free time. This will require greater effort and involvement on your part. I know parents who take their son sailing, belong to the same rambling club and theatre club, and the father coaches him in tennis. However, once your teenagers are old enough to go off on their own, they will see who they like and there won't be much you can do about it.

Should your child want to break away from a certain friend or group but is scared to do so, you can help by telling him to use you. He can say, Mum (or Dad) says I have to stay in, or spend more time on homework, or wants me to join the squash club with them. It gives him a way of escape which his peers can hardly blame on him.

In your home, no matter what, you must remain in control. You do not have to make concessions to accommodate certain friends if you choose not to. Stand by your values and beliefs; you do not have to defend them to anyone. If you always say grace at the table you don't have to omit this because Gary's friend, who is coming to tea, thinks it's stupid.

COMPROMISE

It sounds like a frightening word, but sometimes, when we face open defiance or opposition, compromise may be the only solution. You can't lock a sixteen-year-old in his bedroom! Your son may tell you that his mates are going to an all-night party and he wants to go too. Your instinct tells you, *This doesn't feel right*; he has never stayed out all night before and you don't know the teenagers involved, except perhaps for one. If he isn't allowed to go he is going to feel resentful, angry, and humiliated. So you may have to use compromise. You agree that you will ring the owner of the house first to ensure it is okay. He promises not to drink too much or be tempted to try drugs. You agree that if things get rough he can ring you any time and you will pick him up; also that he is home next morning at an agreed time.

This may sound drastic, he may try to manipulate you, but he'll know you care and that if he's to go, then he has to abide by your rules. Also, if things do go frighteningly wrong he won't be scared to call for help. At eighteen or nineteen he will probably be able to manage, but at sixteen you are still responsible for him.

Not all new experiences are necessarily of a frightening nature; often allowing your child to go to something that appears way-out or daring will take away the compelling urge to rebel.

Having to perform rituals or dares before being allowed to become part of a certain group has been in existence for thousands of years. Adults still get involved in this way. So long as they are freely entered into, do not involve mutilation or self-abuse in any way, do not break the law, and do not take away free will, they are probably quite harmless.

However, as we hear more about new cults starting up, our children do need to be kept aware. Adolescents and young adults are so impressionistic and idealistic it is hard to protect them. Something which, on the surface, seems revolutionary, wonderful, and spiritual, may have a very different side.

The message behind all this is: keep yourself informed, listen to your teenager, encourage friends home (at least you will know where they are and what they are doing), trust them until you are proven wrong and allow them to make mistakes.

6 Making Rules Work and When to Say No!

Sick to death of nagging? Fed up with making rules that are ignored? Feeling that no one is listening to you and that you have lost control? Join the club, for the majority of parents go through this stage before things are worked out.

Rebellion is part of growing up. And yes, teenage children do appear very selfish – it would be hard indeed for them to leave home and get on with their own lives if they focused on how you were feeling. Being self-centred most of the time enables the adolescent to break away.

I have a friend who, after his first baby was born (both he and his wife were only nineteen when they married) decided to emigrate to Australia. He now tells me, with new-found insight, 'I never considered for a moment how our families would feel or how much they would miss seeing their first grandchild grow up.'

Helen told me how teenage for her was a nightmare because her parents never removed or adjusted barriers. Until she married and left home she had to be in by ten every night, was never allowed to choose her own clothes, and had to play with her younger sister. No wonder she married early, and it wasn't surprising that her marriage didn't last. She had never been allowed the right to learn by experimenting; she had never made her own mistakes or found out her strengths and weaknesses.

I see children of all ages pushing against rules and restrictions. This is absolutely normal. How else are they to discover their world from a personal perspective? This doesn't mean we let them fall down the stairs as they learn to climb them, or that we allow them to eat something poisonous in order to discover that it is bad for them.

Because we love our children and have a responsibility towards them, we have to make rules, and certain behaviours have to be stopped or restricted. From the initial control that enables them to survive, we have to teach them to live within a society; this again will become part of their protection. We have to teach them to respect other people's property as well as their own. By our own example we pass our values on to them.

Your first teenager has the toughest time because you are learning how to be a parent. What time he should be in at night, at what age you allow him to go to an all-night party, how you insist on homework being done, and when the TV gets switched off, are all rules that will have been worked out by the time younger brothers and sisters reach adolescence.

Not all children are the·same. Although they have to go through the same physical and emotional changes they often cope with them differently, and rules that work for one may not be appropriate for another. You may have a son who never wants to go to a party and a daughter who thinks her life will end if she isn't allowed to go. Appearance may not matter in the slightest to one and yet be of the utmost importance to another. Talking with your teenagers and *really* listening will help you to make the right rules and decisions at various stages in their development.

COMMUNICATION

Where most relationships fail there is usually a communication problem; almost everyone will either rush to defend themselves or to attack when they experience criticism or opposition. When this happens there can be no communication. You must practise *active listening*, by which process you really hear and intelligently digest what is being said *before* you respond. It is extremely difficult, but it is worth the effort and will prevent a great deal of conflict. Having considered your child's point of view, you then have the right to express your own. You may still decide to disagree, insist that things are done your way, point out the flaws in their thinking, but you should have them listening.

Unless you have an extremely compliant child, or one who is terrified of you, one of the most persistent cries you will hear is, 'Why can't I?' Many parents short-cut the answer with, 'Because I say so'. There will be times when that will be all you have time for, but if you want a thinking responsive child you will need to explain. As your children approach teenage, this will become more and more necessary. Although your rules and requirements may be met with sulks or argument, at least they will *know* why you tell them they may not go to a rave-up, wear high-heeled shoes to school, play loud pop music after eleven at night ...

If you don't always know the answers and need to think them through, you can always use delaying tactics: 'We'll talk about it later', or 'I'll discuss it with your father'. You may find that sometimes the things you are requiring of them are no longer necessary or appropriate.

There will be safety rules your child may flaunt which will have your hair standing up on end, and there will be nothing you can do about it.

If your teenager's behaviour results in contact with the law and it is handled well, it may prove to be one of the best things that can happen. Your role is to support the law and to show the respect your child needs to cultivate. Calling the police 'pigs', or breaking the law yourself, is not going to help your child.

It is no use telling your child, 'You have to look after yourself in this world', or 'You can never get on if you are honest to the letter'. They won't know the difference between doing something that is a little dishonest and a great big offence. Dishonesty changes *you*, no matter how you try to justify it.

In the days when we kept horses and my children were aged from about two to fourteen, the blacksmith came to shoe a couple of the ponies. Afterwards he asked if he could watch our television for a while; he had backed a couple of horses, and wanted to see them run. We all went indoors and I made him some tea. The telephone rang, and it was someone asking if he was still with us. I turned to George. He shook his head. 'Tell them I've already left,' he said. But I couldn't; I held the receiver out towards him. 'You'll have to tell him yourself,' I told him. As he came towards the phone I noticed my children's faces. All six had been watching me closely, wondering if I would tell a lie.

We have a responsibility to act honestly all the time – it gives our children security, and they know where they stand. Quite rightly, they reason that if you are truthful in *all* your dealings, then they can trust you.

People you see who have done well with their lives have usually got there through their own efforts and not by taking short-cuts, pocketing things that do not belong to them, drinking to excess, skiving off early from work, or treating others with disrespect. They feel good about themselves and what they do.

You will need to sit down from time to time and review things with your teenager. Give him the opportunity to tell how he feels about certain things. You may not have noticed how he has changed. Taking him along to the beach or cinema with his pals is going to have to stop when he starts a 'special' relationship. No boy of sixteen, out with his new girlfriend, wants to be sitting next to his father. As his confidence grows he may choose to bring her to the golf club, the pub or on an outing with you.

Allowing your teenager to borrow the car is another tough decision. Your son may be a very careful driver (but he lacks experience) and your insurance will go up considerably; and can you manage without the car for a while if there is an accident? Giving friends a lift can cause the foot to go down just a little too hard on the accelerator, and stimulating conversation may interfere with concentration. Only you can decide. If you say no, make it clear why and stick by your decision. If you have no public transport and don't care for him to be walking or cycling great distances at night, you may have to become a taxi service for a few years.

At this stage in his life there are areas where he has to be given choices. You may like to suggest that you each list those things that directly affect you both and then discuss your lists together. This gives him an opportunity to tell you things he hasn't perhaps known how to broach before.

Your list may look something like this:

- Money
- Invasion of my privacy
- Disregard for my rules
- Drinking alcohol to excess
- Wasting educational opportunities
- Fear of causing an unwanted pregnancy (or in the case of a daughter, becoming pregnant)
- Rows and conflict

Be prepared for a few shocks when you see your teenager's list – it may look something like this:

- You giving my friends the third degree when they visit
- Talking about me to the neighbours
- Telling me how I should spend my money
- Going into my room
- Waiting up for me when I'm late home
- Always comparing your teenage with mine
- Nagging me to study
- Interfering with my life

Don't prejudge your teenager; let him talk to you about why he feels the way he does, and consider his points of view before leaping in to defend your position.

You might, as an alternative, start by both agreeing to list three things about each other that really gets to you. These may

include you nagging about his clothes, criticizing his friends, setting what he sees as unreasonable limits. This may cause you to
rethink certain rules and to question whether they are realistic
or justified.

It is all right to express your feelings too. If you get upset,
angry, distressed, worried over something, you can say so. Your
intention in doing this should not be to make your teenager feel
guilty but to promote understanding and co-operation. If he is
coming home too late, tell him why you worry.

The brick wall

A lady client came to see me because she was extremely depressed over her three children – all teenagers. She said she
couldn't talk to them about anything. They refused to listen or
to co-operate, were rude, and did not consider that she had any
feelings. 'I might as well bang my head against a brick wall,' she
told me. It must surely have felt that way, for one of her problems was severe headaches and migraine.

She was divorced and had virtually no contact with the father
of her children. As she talked, I realized that she had many
problems of her own that, unwittingly, she was passing on to her
family. She was also using her children to work through problems that went back to her own childhood. But right now she
wanted immediate help in what she saw as an impossible situation. She is not alone. Many parents feel they are wasting breath
even trying to reach their children; their behaviour is unruly,
outrageous, insolent.

I told her: In your home you do have rights. You can make
rules that are reasonable and are going to affect the way the rest
of the family survive. Your teenagers may not like it, but if they
are going to continue to live there they must learn to respect
your property, your space and your values. The fewer rules made
the more likely they are to have the desired effect. If they keep
the rest of the house or apartment free from their clutter, then a

rule that their bedrooms are cleaned once a week is a good compromise. If they don't, then they should know the outcome. It is best to try and agree between you what is fair and what privileges will be withdrawn. In their bedroom, for example: you can decide that if they don't keep it clean you will go in once a week and blitz it, which means they lose the rights of privacy (the magazines under the bed will be turfed out); or they lose TV watching rights for a week; or they are grounded until it's done; or they don't get to play rugby or baseball on Saturday. You will have to work out between you a deterrent that actually does work, and see that it is carried through when they don't keep to the agreement.

But then I know someone whose son said he didn't care if she took away the TV, stopped him going out, or did the room herself. If they are still young enough, a *Do it now! Because I say so!* will suffice. However, this can be exhausting and is not the best way long-term. With teenagers you have to stand by what you have said, and enforce the rules.

PUNISHMENT

Before condemning your children, make sure of the facts. You could be wrong. Now my own are grown, what they recall most clearly are the two occasions when they were punished for something they had *not* done. They felt that punishment for crimes they had committed was fair and justified. I do believe, however, that deterrents are preferable to punishment.

Modern theory does now lean very heavily towards remoulding and not punishment. This is fine in theory, but from experience I know that if punishment is only used on very rare occasions – when it really matters – it is a very effective way of getting over a message.

By the time your children have become adolescents, punishment is no longer appropriate, and withdrawal of privileges is more effective. There will be opposition to this, but if you have agreed in advance and stick to those rules you shouldn't encounter too much rebellion.

Being constant at all times will help more than perhaps you can imagine. Rules need to be supported by both parents. If you do not get the back-up of the other parent the message to your children is that it is not important. Making our rules and sticking to them enables them to know where they stand. It is also preparation for the big world outside where they are going to have to learn to respect other people's property and rights.

It can be tough on single parents who do not have back-up and seem always to be the one making rules and 'going-on' at them. Where you have the support of a grandparent or mature friend whom your teenager respects, you may ask them to talk with your child; this way he won't feel the situation is completely one-sided. Many teenagers choose an adult confidant outside the family; this can be a bonus and can work well.

If you really can't cope, seek professional advice before things get too bad. Schools and colleges have counsellors, house masters (or mistresses) who will know your child and should be made aware of any real problems.

Don't weaken

There are many times when you will have to dig in your heels, stand up for your own rights and what you believe in, protect your own space, and exercise the right to change your mind occasionally.

If you have allowed something to happen in your teenager's life and it hasn't worked, tell him: 'Yes, I know we let you go to Jody's party last time, but you drank too much, came home and were sick all over the bathroom floor. You may have learned better, but I don't think you are ready yet to cope with the pressures of everyone else at those kind of parties. The answer is, *No*. We'll review the situation next time around.' He won't like it, but then he isn't going to like everything you say or do. Being unpopular from time to time is part of parenting.

Every child I have ever known does, at least occasionally, use emotional blackmail. They tell you they will lose their friends if they aren't allowed to . . . Or that you are spoiling their lives and this thing they just have to do will only happen once, and that they won't ask again. They may be outwardly defiant, 'You can't stop me, anyhow.' Don't believe it! If they think that their lives depend on one event then they have other problems they need to address. Saying no sometimes won't spoil their lives, but not caring enough to make rules that have to be respected will.

Encouraged by the behaviour of friends, your daughter may pressurize you by saying, 'Julia's Mum lets her go, I can stay at Dean's the night, you don't have to worry.' Where other friends are concerned, check it out. If your child swears this will cause her to die of embarrassment, or that she will never be asked again, point out that it is courteous to speak to the parents first. They may not know their son plans to have a party (your daughter may know this too!).

I know parents who make it a rule that no friends are allowed into the house while they are out. This may sound drastic, but when the mother came home unexpectedly one day and found her thirteen-year-old lighting a fire in the loft with his friend, drastic action had to be taken. 'I'm sure you didn't think of the consequences,' his mother said. 'Until you are a bit older and able to think ahead in a more responsible manner, there will be no more friends in the house unless your father or I are home.'

A mother of two teenage sons, who has had a hard struggle controlling them, due partly to an ex-husband who does not support her way of bringing up the boys, has made the following ground rules.

1 If you break the law I will go to the police.
2 If you bring drugs into the house you are out.
3 You will contribute towards the cost of food and accommoda-

tion or find somewhere else to live (they are both employed).

4 You will not have sex with your girlfriends in the house – it embarrasses me.

5 You will take your share of doing the chores (she does try to give them ones they don't mind doing too much).

6 You are responsible for keeping your own bedroom clean (she doesn't care how tidy it is but insists on a level of hygiene that has been agreed between them).

7 You will respect my rights to do what I want in my home.

She also tells them that they may come and talk to her about anything, and promises not to prejudge. All this has taken time to sort out. One has left home twice and come back; one has experimented with drugs. She has found the older one in bed with his girlfriend and didn't like her own response so decided she didn't have to put up with it.

The important thing is that they now know where they stand. They are still often rude, cheeky, and sometimes sulk. When they are slack over their chores, she simply doesn't present the expected meal and they have to get their own. 'It sounds tough,' she said, 'But I have had to learn to do what is in their best interests long-term.' She says she wishes she had the wisdom to have made these rules years ago, but she didn't have the experience that can only come from growing with your children into teenage.

I think her rules are good. You may like to make some with your own children, probably the sooner the better. If they are only 13 you can hardly throw them out, so that threat is not appropriate, and you will have to work out something else that has the desired effect.

Asking a local policeman to have a chat to younger teenagers may work. This is not going too far if it puts a stop to some really serious behaviour. I have known it work with youngsters who had stolen but were too young to be taken to court. Getting them involved in any activity which involves discipline, such as a team sport, is good. Helping them fulfil a dream brings their focus onto something worthwhile and they see you as an ally and are thus more inclined to co-operate.

It is a fact that young people who are busy are far less likely to get into serious trouble.

LOSING CONTROL

Instead of panicking when you feel you are losing control, consider passing over control for certain things. Make your teenagers responsible for getting to school or work on time; if they are late it may be the only way for them to learn that the one who suffers as a consequence is themselves. The same applies to homework and studies. But I can't let them ruin their lives, you may protest. Neither can you stop them, for it is their life and they will, ultimately, have to handle it their way. Sometimes young people need to do wild irrational things, like spending all their money on a leather jacket and having none left to pay bus fares to college, before they get it right.

At those times, when nothing seems to be working, it is possibly a wise move to review your own thinking and intentions: 'Why do I feel like this about ... ?' may give you a new insight. Is it because you know of someone who had this problem and ended up in jail? Does it actually remind you of something that happened to you at that age? Perhaps you were home late and were molested or frightened – that is no reason to prevent your daughter being out after dark, but you should equip her to cope if threatened by such an incident. Personal alarms are a great comfort and deterrent, and so is learning self-defence. Useful tips include: walk home with someone else; try to keep to streets that are lighted; walk with confidence (evidence shows that this is a very effective way of protecting oneself); wear low-heeled shoes (so that they can run if they have to). Boys have similar problems, so make sure that appropriate precautions are also

Keeping control also includes your own ability to keep things in perspective

taken with sons. Security alarms can be clipped to the belt or put in the pocket. Carrying an alarm does not turn them into sissies; many men now have them.

Keeping control also applies to your own ability to keep things in perspective. When your teenager is very late home it is natural to start to worry. Before an hour has passed you are probably imagining that all kinds of terrible things have happened: rape, beaten-up, victim of a car accident. We are bombarded with horror stories from the media, and begin to believe that the whole world has become a bad place. Although this is not so, recent changes for the worst in our society cannot be ignored. In some countries children can still play alone out in the streets, or wander through the countryside on their bicycles; in others this is no longer advisable. At what age your child is safe to go out alone is something you will decide depending on the maturity of the child and where you live.

It is the responsibility of everyone to help make the world a safer place for our children. Many authorities, including local councils, schools and the police, are now actively trying to do this, and they need your co-operation. Finding out more and taking an active part will have an effect. Youth centres and youth opportunity schemes, summer camps, adventure playgrounds, sports centres, neighbourhood watch, all welcome voluntary help and positive input. Should you see something you suspect is not right, investigate or report it. In this way you are helping to take back control.

You may find it hard to say 'No' to your children's friends always being in your house because you were never allowed to have friends in when you were a child. Should this be happening to you, let it surface and try to get things into perspective. You don't *have* to be a 'Yes' parent all the time; you don't have to give in, be a slave, buy everything your child wants in order to be liked or loved. Saying 'No' when you believe this is the right thing to do can be a definite step forward rather than a retrograde one.

Some people believe that expecting children to help in the home is wrong. They think children have to cope with all that when they grow up, and should simply be allowed to enjoy the freedom of childhood. The fact is that this doesn't work. A child's sense of self-esteem and self-worth develops when they are included and allowed to help. It also equips them for the future. Preparing the dinner sometimes, helping in the garden, ironing their own shirts, assures them that they can look after themselves.

You may find you are faced with comparison: *Josie's Mum let's her stay out until eleven; Pete never has to clean his room; What does it matter if my jeans are dirty? Ian always wears his like this and his parents never go on at him.* Yes, but this is *your* home and you like things done differently. So long as your rules are reasonable you should not have too great a battle – and perhaps, not even one at all!

If your child is still living at home by the time he reaches twenty it is probably time to help him into the outside world. Nothing is going to be of more value to him than actually learning he can make it without his parents.

Another area of control concerns your own emotional responses. Getting angry, yelling, or using physical violence only teaches violence or causes intimidation – long-term this does not produce a well-balanced adult. If you do have problems in this area and can't find a better way of handling things, backing off a bit and allowing your spouse to take more responsibility for the control may be the solution. Where there is no partner, or yours does not feel able to take on additional responsibility for discipline, another way is to seek outside help from trusted friends or relatives. Many people on a short fuse are experiencing too much stress; they may be very worried over something, they may have a physical problem such as high blood pressure or over-active thyroid; they may never have recognized that there is a better way of getting co-operation. Don't rule out the possibility of seeking help for yourself; counselling is now well-recognized as being more effective in many areas than doling out anti-depressants or similar drugs.

Lack of control can also be exhibited in people who become easily upset, burst into tears, develop a headache, or take to their beds when things get out of hand. This can make a teenager very frustrated, guilty, withdrawn, or resentful. Our teenage children *are* going to make us aware of our own shortcomings; we can use this as an opportunity to grow as a human being and to find better responses and solutions.

Our teenager's behaviour and responses are often reflections of our own. If we don't like what we are witnessing, is it possible that we are seeing something that we do not like within ourselves? One may say, 'I don't want Philip to grow up like me (or his father)', and then try to push him in another direction. This kind of action usually doesn't achieve much, unless he sees for himself that becoming an alcoholic like his father is foolish. Better to deal with your own problem by taking positive action. 'I don't want you to become a soak like me, son. It's a fool's game. So I've decided to do something about it' – and *you do*. This is a far better way than simply telling them, 'Don't make the mistakes I made.'

The same applies to smoking. It is no use telling your child not to do something that you persist in doing.

The good news is that most teenagers recognize the value of rules, and that they allow them to live safely and in harmony with others. If we didn't all drive on the same side of the road there would be chaos; if we dumped our rubbish out on the sidewalk there would soon be rats and disease; if we didn't uphold the law nobody would be safe.

Sometimes the only way they are really going to learn is to leave home. It can be quite an eye-opener to visit your son or daughter for the first time in their own place and discover how clean and tidy it is.

Some mothers, to whom tidiness is so important or who can't relax, may choose to clear up the chaos themselves, or put everything that is left out in a large sack or bin. I used to do this with socks – I became so fed up with trying to sort them out, I simply gave up, put them all together, and left the family to deal with them. I made it their problem and not mine.

Making rules about the time that your teenager has to be in will depend a lot on where they are and what is happening the next day. Homework should be a priority; staying out later when they do not have to go to school next day is more reasonable than insisting they are always home by a set time.

Staying up all night is, for some reason, considered to be the grown-up thing to do. I recall one night when my teenage son was entertaining friends downstairs and the noise was keeping me awake I decided I had to do *something*. I didn't want to embarrass him or nag, so I slipped quietly downstairs and removed a fuse. Being plunged into darkness and unable to play their music worked like magic; within minutes the visitors were on their way out and I was able to return to bed with a chuckle and settle down to sleep. When I admitted my 'crime' the next day, he saw the funny side of it, and I actually went up in his estimation for the inventive way I had solved the problem.

If you are worried that a party held in your house is going to cause havoc, put your teenager and a friend in charge. Making someone responsible really does help keep things under control.

When my friend's daughter first had a moped, she was very much against letting her parents know where she was going and what time she would be home, even though they explained that if she had an accident and ended up in a ditch they wouldn't know where to begin looking for her. When she moved out to share a flat with a friend, her mother overheard her say to some-one: 'We always tell each other where we are going to be on the safe side; you never know what might happen.'

Oh yes! They will learn, so don't despair; it's just that they don't like being told.

7   Sex and Relationships

Relationships come before sexual involvement; learning how to handle yourself, what to expect, how to communicate, building confidence, making choices, and being able to say 'No', are all part of natural development. Although one of our greatest concerns is what will happen to our children when they become sexually active, we can avoid many of the things we most fear by ensuring that they are well informed.

Fifty years ago parents seldom talked to their children about sex, and it was not part of the school curriculum. Most knowledge of the subject came from friends or older siblings, and often it was incorrect or very limited. I can recall going into public toilets and crouching above the lavatory seat because Mother had said we must never to sit on it; we never knew why, and she never told us. The notice on the door with messages about VD was something else mysterious and never talked about; perhaps she thought this information was something we were never going to need. (And, by the way, you really can't catch Sexually Transmitted Diseases – STD – by sitting on a toilet seat.)

Now, with the very real possibility of coming into contact with STD, Aids and HIV, it is imperative that our children are kept informed. Although the medical world knows far more about these diseases than even ten years ago, they are still on the increase. The fact is that if your child is sexually active he or she is at risk; the only way to guarantee 100 per cent safety is by total abstinence. This is not very likely when you hear that by the age of eighteen more than half of all young people will have had at least one sexual encounter.

Talking to your children early on, before they embark on any relationships, is the best way of protecting them. They need to know exactly what happens, how to use protection, how to recognize when something is wrong, and what action to take. Most children are told too late and have either started experimenting, or have already formed their own ideas.

I do not think it is wise or necessary to talk to seven-year-olds about oral sex, contraception, or Aids, unless they ask. Their innocence and the right to grow up without having to take on extra knowledge (and fear) that isn't necessary or appropriate for their present needs seems cruel to me. But you will have to make that decision for yourself.

By the age of eleven or twelve all children should know about sex and the risks involved in becoming sexually active. They need to be made aware before their bodies begin to change. If you really feel you can't talk to them, get a good book for them to read, and then use it as a point of discussion afterwards. If you love your children, you are going to have to overcome any feelings of embarrassment.

Some people argue that things have changed so much since they were that age that they don't know what to tell their children – well, you can always find out.

RELATIONSHIPS

Consciously or unconsciously we are all searching for fulfilment, and our needs are many; the way in which various people fulfil these needs determines a relationship. Our first and most important experience of a relationship is with our mother; this is our learning place. As we develop our needs change, and father and then other members of the family begin to play an important role. Gradually, we begin to look outside for different relationships to satisfy new needs.

Sometimes we can feel very lonely, not recognizing we have a need which is not being met. We have a deep fundamental need to be loved and understood, and as we grow our parents can no longer satisfy us. We make new friends and include more people in our lives to satisfy growing needs – emotional, intellectual, physical and spiritual – and when they are all fulfilled we become whole.

Sometimes you may only need one loving person in your life; more often we need a variety of people to whom we can relate. A boy will find that a girlfriend cannot fulfil his need for masculine company, and so has to be part of the football club; a girl may find she needs a female friend when she goes shopping for clothes, or wishes to confide in someone. Tying yourself down exclusively to one person can become stifling and psychologically unhealthy.

During our development we begin to have the need of a partner, a special friend, someone with whom we can share in a special way. Children usually pick a 'best friend' at school within the first year of attending. Gradually they expand their horizons and experience different relationships. There is often a very special relationship between grandparents and grandchildren. The strong feelings we get for a teacher, pop star, or some remote older person is the prelude to being directly involved with someone. Having a 'crush' on someone can be a lovely safe way of playing with your feelings.

Eventually, fulfilment of needs sought in a relationship will include sex; it is natural and cannot be denied. Your son or daughter will begin to look for someone of the opposite sex to satisfy this need. They may not be aware of this for a long time, and they may try hard to convince you it is just a pal; they have still to recognize their own sexuality.

In the past we have tried to tell our children to wait until they are married before becoming sexually involved, convinced that this was the best way to lasting happiness. Few would now agree. At the same time, living together before marriage has certainly resolved nothing, for more people than ever before are separating or getting divorced. Marriage is a commitment for life. By encouraging your child to have a number of friends of the opposite sex you will help her to find out about herself and what she does ultimately want in a lifelong partner.

I feel very strongly that we should stress the importance of love and caring when talking to our children about sex, although these seem to be rarely spoken about any more in sex education.

When your teenager decides what she wants from a relationship, and that this does include feelings of love, tenderness and caring, she will feel a lot safer and avoid many heartaches. Being good friends with a boy doesn't mean that she will lose him unless she goes to bed with him. Having been taught to value her body, she will be better able to choose carefully before committing herself to someone in that way, and this will give some protection against disillusionment or feeling used.

This doesn't imply that boys are only after sex (though some may be). Just as some girls seek out the physical experience through curiosity, or through the need to be accepted without the emotional commitment, so boys can feel as deeply and intensely as girls.

Young people who deny emotional feelings have usually been very hurt or rejected at some time – possibly by one or both parents. They should be encouraged to express their feelings without the burden of guilt or repercussions. This may be best achieved through counselling or group family therapy.

Taking time to build a relationship is very rewarding. Waiting for, and then receiving that first kiss can be a magical moment that will never be forgotten. However, passion is very powerful and people can literally be swept off their feet. They may know what they are doing is unwise, they may tell themselves that they hardly know this person, but it makes no difference. To make love *now* seems to be the only thing they can do; later, regrettably, they may well wish that they had not allowed themselves to be carried away by their feelings.

TALKING ABOUT SEX

Survival is the most powerful of all forces and this includes per-petuating the species; this energy is what enables us to survive. Controlling this drive is one of the most difficult and essential things that we, as human beings, have to learn to do. Over-population, using up natural resources, passing on disease and handicaps, having more children than we can support, are our responsibility. However, when you are fourteen, or sixteen, or even twenty, you are still learning all about responsibility.

Although sex education is now taught in most countries, your children will still need to know how *you* feel about things, and also what you think is right and wrong. Practise using the correct words; penis, vagina and breasts should not be taboo and yet, somehow, it feels easier to use slang. Make a joke about some-thing and it's easier to talk about it.

In much the same way as a baby learns about his world by reaching out to touch things, the adolescent wants to experience sex, and it is vital that you prepare her for it in a sensitive and yet practical way. For example, when you talk with your teenager about sex, suggest that she tries, before things go too far, to ask her-self, *Are we ready for this yet?* and, *Do we have adequate protection?*

Some people still believe they cannot become pregnant under certain conditions, or at certain times, because of all kinds of old wives' tales. The truth is that you can get pregnant *at any time*; you do not have to be a homosexual to get Aids; to believe you are safe because your partner swears he/she has never had sex with anyone else is asking for trouble.

Explain what condoms are, and why it is important that they are used; they are the safest way of having sex. Your child may have already learned all this at school but it doesn't hurt to let her know that you know too, and that she can talk to you about such things. This doesn't have to be done in such a way as to indicate that you assume she is about to become sexually active. You can explain that this is a way in which responsible people protect themselves and their partners.

The girl is as responsible as the boy for taking precautions. The cap, at present, is considered one of the safest ways of protection against disease; it creates a barrier and so offers protection against cervical cancer, which is more likely to develop if she is sexually active from an early age. The coil has lost its popularity since it has been found to cause pelvic inflammation in some women.

The contraceptive pill is a convenient alternative, but does not guard against STD, and its use is now being questioned because of the side-effects of certain brands. At the time of writing one in five 16 and 17-year-olds use the Pill. Evidence suggests that the Pill gives some protection against ovarian and womb cancers, pelvic infections and cysts. However, antibiotics and some other drugs can interfere with its effectiveness, so those on the Pill should check with their doctor in such cases.

To be totally protected it is necessary to use a condom as well as the Pill, and one in four teenagers are reported as doing so. You can help in providing these for your son or daughter; if they know there are some on the bathroom shelf and that they can go and get them without having to ask permission, they are much more likely to use them. If they are going to have sex anyway, make it safe – and if you think a free supply of condoms is expensive, imagine the cost financially (and to your freedom) if a baby does arrive and your daughter has no means of taking on that responsibility herself. This does not mean that you are condoning what your adolescent is doing – you may disapprove strongly. Providing you speak openly about your feelings on the matter, the supply of condoms will not be seen as a sign of encouragement but will indicate that you care about your adolescent's well-being and happiness. Hard to do, perhaps, but we are talking about a life here, and more than one life will be affected if Aids or some other disease results from unprotected sex.

As your child grows older and earns his own money, or is given an allowance, he should pay for condoms himself. This is part of the commitment to growing up and taking responsibility.

Listen to what your adolescents have to say about sex and relationships. They may know more than you do, and may have already decided not to get involved until they are in a long-term relationship or married. They may simply not be ready yet. I know quite a few young people who have passed through their teens and never had a girlfriend or boyfriend. This does not mean they are homosexual or that there is something wrong with them; some haven't found the right partner, and others are too shy to actually date someone.

Make it absolutely clear to your daughter that no matter how far petting has gone, she always has the right to say 'No' to intercourse. Many girls think that because they have allowed things to go so far they cannot tell the boy to stop. It is safer, however, to stop things before they become too intimate. Where they have strong beliefs about their body, virginity, or only having sex when they are married, they should say so.

Most young people do not have a very satisfactory sex life at first; as with everything, they have to learn how to please and what pleases. Their first experiences will have come through touching their own bodies, masturbating and wet dreams (emissions of semen during sleep). Beginning to know how their bodies work and how they respond still has to be communicated to the person with whom they are having sex. This isn't always easy. Those boys who boast the loudest are often the ones still floundering. The shift from self-pleasuring to sharing is part of learning to put other people's feelings at least on a level with your own.

If you have strong religious beliefs, or standards that do not permit sexual activities before marriage, you need to discuss these with your teenager. They may not go along with the way you think, but you will have explained why you believe sex outside marriage is wrong. Whatever they then decide to do, it should not become a burden of guilt, or kept secret because of what you think.

A friend of mine spoke recently on this subject. 'My husband would go mad if he knew our son was no longer a virgin,' she said. (The boy is 19, at university, and sharing accommodation with a girlfriend.) 'He would never allow him in our house again.' Here the mother is caught up in a conspiracy that prevents her being honest. If you truly love your child, you should be able to accept him without condemning him out of hand because his beliefs differ from your own.

If you have a good open relationship with your children, they should be able to ask you for the answers to questions that are bothering them. If you don't know what to say there are plenty of informative books around. A couple of books on sex in the house doesn't mean that you have entered into pornographic reading.

FEELINGS AND THE WAY ADOLESCENTS SEE THEMSELVES

Sex isn't simply about the act of creation; it involves feelings at many levels. Many things that happened way back in our childhood can affect the way we cope with our feelings, and how we view ourselves as human beings. Many teenagers develop hangups from childhood experiences that result in such a poor selfimage that they can't believe anyone could love them or find them desirable.

Your daughter may start using far more make-up than you think is seemly or sensible, and the clothes she wants to wear may appear too sexy and likely to invite trouble. Guidance is necessary in cases like this; you do need to protect your daughter from advances she is not yet ready to handle. But she too is struggling to make a statement of her individuality; dressing-up is a way of telling the world she is no longer a child, and she certainly doesn't want to be laughed at by her contemporaries. Guidance needs to be given without damaging her self-esteem. It is worth reminding yourself from the time to time that although your teenager appears to have complete disregard for your opinions she still needs reassurance, and what you think *does matter*.

The underlying message of independence may demonstrate itself in a change of clothing, hair style, wanting to wear make-up or unusual jewellery (nose rings and so on). Young people almost always want to be different to their parents; they want to be seen as individuals with their own personalities, likes and dislikes; choosing a life style that says *This is me!* is one way of doing this. They definitely do *not* want to be seen as little clones of their parents any longer. Perceived as rejection, this makes the parent fight to prevent change, afraid of where all this is leading. Seen for what it really is, you can encourage change in the right direction without feeling you have failed, or that you have lost control.

You may tell your teenager to look around at all the happily married people, and at relationships where the people are far from 'perfect', but that makes little difference. They can only see the way they believe they look, and that is often terrible. It is totally irrational to expect people to fit a set of figures and formulae that have become accepted as beautiful, but emotions are not rational and are far more powerful than logic. Unless your daughter can be slim, have perfect teeth and the right-sized bust, she may think life isn't worth living. If your son cannot be six feet tall, have every muscle in exactly the right place, hard and bulging, he won't believe any girl will look at him.

I have tried asking some young people to consider their close friends, and to ask themselves whether they like them because of the way they look or because of the way they are – but it doesn't work. They still believe that to be acceptable, liked and loved, *they* have to possess the perfect body.

If your teenager has other skills that are admired, she may not be so caught up in this illusion, but unfortunately most are, and breaking that concept is going to depend on us. If *we* put too much emphasis on appearance it will reinforce their beliefs. Yet so often we still do. We moan about their dress, their hair style, the rings through their noses; so long as they are clean we should try to keep quiet about the 'in-thing' they are currently representing. It almost always passes.

Happiness is a most elusive quality. We believe if only this or that would happen we would be perfectly happy. It doesn't work that way, and it won't work that way for your children either. So if you think that they have everything and ought to be both grateful and happy, then you have forgotten how it feels to be that age. Emotions are going to soar up and down like a yo-yo.

Sometimes being miserable is an experience they need. Teenagers will wallow for a while in extreme feelings; it is how they find out about themselves. This is all right so long as it doesn't continue for too long. If your teenager is depressed for more than a few days, is constantly angry or silent, you need to try and find out why. If you are unable to break through to her, ask one of her friends to find out. Sometimes it is easier to talk to a friend (or grandparent) than to Mum or Dad.

Often our children don't confide in us because they don't believe we can understand. We need to learn to resist butting in, offering advice, telling them how we coped in such a situation. Most of the time when they choose to talk they simply want you to understand, not to give a sermon.

Remember, exaggerated feelings are quite normal. If your teenager tells you she will never get over a broken relationship, she really does believe this. Be patient and understanding, you know that we can get over anything in time and with the right attitude, but she still has to learn this.

Never underestimate your teenager's feelings. Falling in love is a powerful emotion, difficult enough for adults to handle, let alone adolescents. How well did you cope with your emotions as a teenager? Sometimes it is wise for us to recall our own difficulties at that age.

Teenagers rarely believe they are attractive, and getting sexually involved is, for them, a way of convincing themselves that they are not freaks. Before we read the riot act we should consider this. It explains why some teenagers allow themselves to be exploited.

HOMOSEXUALITY

The realization that your child is homosexual can be painful and traumatic for both the adolescent and the parent. There may be feelings of guilt, fear, shame, rejection, loneliness, disbelief, anger and disgust.

The facts about homosexuality have been swept under the carpet for too long. Oscar Wilde was imprisoned for it and not allowed to see his children. Society has moved on a bit since those times, but not much.

There are two reasons why people find those of the same sex attractive to them. One is the way they are made – the balance of hormones responsible are different to those in heterosexual people – the other is psychological.

Most clients I have seen who are homosexual don't wish to change; they simply want to be able to cope with the animosity and ridicule of people who find them unacceptable. They are rarely looking for quick sexual satisfaction, but for a long-term loving relationship.

A lesbian, who had tried living with a man only to find she couldn't make it work, set up home with a girlfriend as her partner. When her mother found out she was appalled. 'Why?' she demanded. Before the girl could stop herself she cried, 'Because you never loved me!' She was seeking a relationship which could provide the female love that she felt had never been there for her.

I knew a man who had five sisters, and was playing at dressing-up when his father returned home and caught him in a dress and wearing high-heeled shoes. In anger he told the son, 'Do that again and I'll send you to school dressed as a girl.' He was frightened of his father, and had noticed how differently his sisters were treated. This was when he made the unconscious decision to become a girl – he felt safer. Girls had a better deal, or so he thought!

Recently I met a man in his seventies who told me that all his life he had felt like a woman in a man's body. He had married and had a child, but still experienced those feelings which he had tried, for most of his life, to deny.

We now know that a certain region of the hypothalamus is much denser in women than in men; this part of the brain has also been found to be smaller in homosexual men than in heterosexuals, which may explain why some men are sexually attracted to other men.

Let us not judge others hastily; if your child confides in you that he/she is 'gay', offer support, assure them you still love them and try to understand.

It is often harder for a father than for a mother to accept that their son is homosexual. It isn't your stigma, and it has nothing to do with you the way your adult child decides to live his life. It should make no difference to your loving him. You may think he should deny his feelings and choose a life of sexual abstinence, but you must keep these thoughts to yourself.

SEXUAL IMPOTENCE

This is not often a problem with young men, but where it is, they are going to feel desperate. They certainly need to speak to someone they trust who will not belittle the situation or make fun of them.

A health problem, alcohol, fear, drugs, guilt, feeling in-adequate, being dominated by the female, believing they have a Sexually Transmitted Disease or that they are going to fail, can all result in impotence. Usually it lasts only a short time. An erection is a reflex action; it is not a voluntary occurrence. A man cannot force himself to have one; usually the more he focuses his attention on the state of his penis the less likely he is to succeed.

Girls sometimes suffer from contraction of the walls of the vagina that prevents penetration, and this is usually caused by fear. If an internal examination shows everything to be normal, sex therapy may help resolve the problem.

About half of all cases of impotence have organic or biological causes. When the problem has a psychological foundation the doctor will most likely refer the patient to a sex therapist – they are very knowledgeable, and have a high success rate.

8   Money Matters

GETTING IT RIGHT

Disputes over money can be the cause of more trouble in a family than almost anything else; some families haven't spoken for years because of arguments or misunderstandings over money. It is the root of so many problems because it can give power and enables independence. Baling out your teenager who consistently gets into debt can create tremendous feelings of anger and resentment. Never learning how to manage on a limited budget leaves our children helpless and very vulnerable.

Early training with pocket money can help to prevent disaster later. Selecting certain jobs at home that are paid for, such as baby-sitting, and taking a part-time job while still in full-time education can give your teenager a feeling of independence and helps teach him the value of money.

I once watched a television programme where children were being advised on the potential values of certain possessions. One child, who was around seven years old, was told that an old album of paintings given to her by her grandmother was worth around £10,000. 'That's a lot of money, isn't it?' she asked. She had no idea how much this represented.

In a way, this innocence is wonderful; not yet influenced by money and materialistic things, their lives have a purity we have lost. It is, however, essential that they become aware of the fact that money *does* matter; it can be used for good, but it can also ruin lives.

Most children, at first, believe that things simply materialize out of thin air. As they grow older, and we begin to deny them things, they start to realize that this is not so. Too many sweets, toys or treats are not in their best interests; we have all met obnoxious spoilt children. We have to teach our children that they can't have everything they desire; monetary restrictions help to teach them self-discipline and to be selective. Taking your small child shopping, allowing her to work out the cost of something and to use money you have given her will be the beginning of learning what she can and can't afford.

Sharing the chores around the house should be part of family participation. There are some jobs or errands that you may decide will be paid for, and these will be viewed differently. It is wise to have a rule that unless *all* the jobs on their list are done, there is no pocket money. The jobs come as a package and in this way it avoids the problem of the child selecting only the ones she doesn't mind doing.

When I was working and most of my children were teenagers, I returned home one evening to find them all watching TV with absolutely nothing done. The room looked as if a bomb had hit it; dishes were piled up in the kitchen, and when I reached the bathroom the basin was covered in a thin film of mud. When I protested, one son said, 'It's no good going on at us, Mum. We just don't see it. If you want us to do something, tell us.'

We sat down together and worked out a list, with each child having one job to do six days of the week; the seventh was their day off. They were allowed to swop jobs if they chose, and sometimes they did. Every week the list was alternated, and as there were six children it meant they were not doing the same chores all the time. There were days when their chores were very simple and took only a few minutes: put out the bin bags for collection on Friday; empty the waste bins; peel the potatoes for dinner. At other times they had to clean the bathroom, change the sheets on their beds, wash the kitchen floor, and so on. Because they were all involved there was no resentment, and the system did work.

It may sound incredible that teenage children don't notice mess and dirty dishes, but they often really don't. Their standards, in any case, are going to be different to yours, so making some jobs a source of income can work. Because you have always been there and done those things it is easy to see how you can be taken for granted. Your children don't *mean* to be thoughtless – as mine said, they just don't notice.

In doing jobs at home, the children have the opportunity to learn how to become efficient in their movements and with their time. Not only will the jobs take less time (and so become more profitable) but the experience will also prepare them for life in the outside world.

MANAGING THEIR OWN MONEY

There will come a time when you have to let your child spend her money unwisely. It wasn't important when she only had money for treats, but when she starts buying her own clothes, she will make mistakes and waste money which you may feel could have been better spent. At what age you decide she is ready to handle a clothing allowance, entertainment money or travel expenses, will depend upon your own budget and your teenager's ability. One child at eleven may already be quite capable of doing this; another, at fourteen, can be far from ready.

A half-way agreement can help them learn without too much aggravation. You may agree to let them use an allowance for pleasure clothes while you still provide clothes for school; you may let them budget for presents, holiday spending money, personal luxuries (such as make-up and aftershave), CDs, magazines, and books other than school books.

Whatever you decide, review the system from time to time. Obviously a thirteen-year-old does not need as much money as one of seventeen. And so, as they grow, things will change.

When your daughter gets a part-time job, you will have to

decide whether she keeps all that money or whether part goes towards her keep. This will depend on how much it is and how you view her earnings. Perhaps she keeps it all, but takes on the responsibility of buying more things for herself.

You may not need a contribution towards the house-keeping but your child still needs to learn that she cannot simply spend everything that she earns on herself. In this case you may like to try taking a reasonable portion of the money your child earns and then save it, perhaps without telling her. When she leaves home it can be used to help buy her first home, as a deposit for rent on an apartment or flat, or as help towards college fees.

I firmly believe that you do not help your children at all by never taking anything from them. How are they going to learn to manage money or develop independence if you always step in and provide everything for them? Where you encounter open resentment: 'You don't need it. What do I have to give you money for anyway?', you can use the above arguments to justify your actions.

As your teenager demonstrates her ability to manage her own money, you will be able to give her more responsibility. This experience will be invaluable to her when she does leave home. It is hard enough learning to cope with getting to work or college on time, buying and cooking your own food, cleaning, studying or coping with a first real job, relationships, and an alien environment, without discovering you can't manage your money as well.

I used to say that the only good thing money did was to set you free to do those things you wanted to do. I now realize that there is something more: money gives you the opportunity to develop character. By learning how to handle money you build self-discipline, pre-thinking and organizational skills, patience, how to be unselfish (using your pocket money to buy a younger brother a present and to go without something for yourself is a wonderful learning experience) and, eventually, you learn that money cannot buy you happiness.

It is good advice to tell your teenager to keep a record of how she spends her allowance/pocket money for the month – then, if it really isn't enough, you may have to review the situation. This can be fun and challenging.

When my first three children reached teenage, we moved into an old house in the country which had been turned into two flats. We decided to let the boys, who were by then earning, have the upper flat to themselves. I thought that in this way they could learn all that was entailed in looking after a home and managing their own money while we were still around if they needed help. It was amusing to observe that after they received their first electricity bill they went round replacing the bulbs with lower wattage ones. They started reminding each other to 'Switch off that light' and asking 'Did you leave the water heater on?' All my years of trying to teach them to be economical had had little effect; when the bills became their responsibility they soon sorted this problem out.

The telephone bill is another source of conflict. I resorted to a lock, but many phones nowadays don't lend themselves to this old-fashioned type of security. Some enable you to use a PIN (Personal Identity Number) which is marvellous until an emergency crops up and you are away from home. Itemized bills are a great help, but some only detail calls over a certain amount. Writing down all your calls really doesn't seem to work in most households. My son, who shares his house with three students, finally agreed that the only thing to do was to split the bill four ways. Another family told their daughter she didn't have to make any contribution towards her keep, but they made her responsible for paying the telephone and electricity bills instead – you can't imagine how their bills came down after that!

When Janet, my friend's daughter, started earning, she agreed with her mother on the amount she would contribute towards the house-keeping. After a couple of weeks she asked how much her food cost. When she found this was only two-thirds of the amount she was paying, she looked at her mother aghast and said, 'Then you are trying to make money out of me!' She really didn't think she had to contribute towards the other bills. 'Well, if I wasn't here you would still have most of those,' she said. Years later, when she had left home, she returned to visit and spoke with her younger brother who was still living there. 'You don't know how lucky you are living at home,' she told him. 'I pay just in rent what you pay Mum for everything.' She had learned the real cost of living.

Getting into debt

This shouldn't be a problem until your child goes off to university and needs to arrange a loan, or has an important project that

needs to be financed. It is asking for trouble to arrange a loan, use a credit card, borrow from friends or family unless you know, without a shadow of doubt, that you can repay that debt.

Equally, as parents you should *never lend or guarantee money for your child unless you can afford to lose it.* It is far better to say 'No' from the beginning than to go through the turmoil of trying to get your child to repay a debt, which can cause a breakdown in the best of family relationships. They may have created a dozen other financial commitments that have to be met first, and you may discover you have to sell your shares, car, or even house, to cover a legal guarantee on a project that went hopelessly wrong.

9   Drug and Alcohol Abuse

DRUGS

So much publicity, so many warnings, so many awful sad stories of
addiction and premature deaths due to drugs – how can a parent
prevent this sort of thing happening?

Most parents are wise enough to realize that drugs are now so
readily available that it would be surprising if their child didn't
come into contact with them. We are frightened, perhaps more
than in any other area, that our children might get involved.
How do you safeguard against it? And is it possible to guide your
teenagers through this period of temptation until they are able
to make the right choices for themselves?

First of all, be informed. Know what drugs do, what they look
like, how to recognize when your child gets involved, and know
where to go for help. In almost every town there is now a drug
advisory department; leaflets giving detailed information are also
available from clinics or your doctor. School will be educating
your child on the subject of drugs and their dangers. Do talk
with your child about them; he will need to know that *you*
know, and that he can come to you if he needs help.

He will probably be offered drugs before he reaches teenage.
He may be aware of the dangers, but young people have in-
satiable curiosity, a need for excitement, a longing to try something they consider daring. Peer pressure will also play an
enormous part in driving your child to try drugs. Going to a

party and being the only one *not* indulging makes them conspicuous and appear weak. The reality is that you have to be
strong to resist such pressures. Remind your child of this – he
can use the argument if he needs to.

One of the best ways to protect your child is to have helped
him build a good sense of self-worth. He won't then have the
same need to join in, and will feel confident in making his own
choices. Hopefully, he will know that one of the things that
makes him special is being himself.

Whatever the argument, all drugs are harmful. Anything that
affects your ability to think clearly, make your own decisions, or
influences your behaviour in any way, is potentially dangerous.
Some drugs also damage internal organs and increase the risk of
cancer. Believing they are non-addictive is unrealistic; there is
much evidence to support the fact that most people who start
with 'soft' drugs progress to those that are addictive and can kill.
Drugs can cause confusion, paranoia, apathy, can affect learning
and de-motivate. On a physical level they can inhibit natural
growth and development (including menstruation), and the
residual effects of some drugs in the body can even affect the
next generation.

We all know that smoking has a detrimental effect on an
unborn baby and is more likely to cause miscarriage or premature birth. Many women do stop when they want to become
pregnant (ideally this should happen six months before con-
ception); they have a wonderful motive that becomes more
powerful than their habit. Perhaps we should look at some
achievable goal that would encourage teenagers to stop not only
smoking but also taking drugs.

Who wants to get old anyway? This is an argument that may be
thrown at you as you struggle to persuade your teenager there is
more in life than *now*, and that what they are doing will be greatly
regretted later. They may be experiencing a sense of hopelessness,
a broken romance, no hopes of getting a job, living with parents
who are always arguing. Drugs offer temporary escape.

Students with prospects of a wonderful future and with everything to live for may still get caught up in the drug scene. There are a dozen different reasons why youngsters try them. You may have been ideal parents, given your children security and love, taught them right from wrong, and yet still they try them. A girl or boy may be persuaded to 'Just try this once', and if they happen, at that time, to be hopelessly in love with the one offering the drug, they are quite likely to do so.

Last year a girl came to see me quite desperate for help. Some drug had been slipped into her drink without her knowledge. A while later she started to laugh and could not stop. On the way home a group of them stopped to buy take-away food. While they were waiting she continued to laugh and giggle. She was aware that everyone was staring at her but still could not stop. When she realized afterwards what must have happened she became terrified of drinking anything. In this distressed state she even came to believe the water in the tap could, in some way, have been tampered with.

One of the dangers is that under the influence of some drugs you believe you can achieve anything. Like the person who believes after a few drinks that he is a better driver – it is impossible to reason with people who are on a 'high'.

Most drugs, including alcohol and tobacco, are seen as reducing stress and helping one to relax in a social situation. Drugs are not the answer; the underlying problem, a lack of confidence, needs to be addressed.

Taking drugs is illegal – this may change, but right now if you use drugs you are breaking the law. This in itself makes it daring and more exciting than smoking tobacco. Statistics show, however, that the number of deaths from smoking cigarettes is far higher than from taking alcohol or illegal drugs. So making drugs legal doesn't sound as if it would deter young people from using them. It might even bring down the price.

When the pressures of life seem too much, most people look for a quick fix. A quick drink or drag on a cigarette seems a simple solution, but it can lead to addiction, can cost a lot of money, and doesn't really deal with the problem.

The truth is that drug-taking does make the user feel good – if it didn't the pushers would soon be out of business. Drugs can make people feel wonderfully happy, excited or calm. Some people become addicted to the emotional response to certain drugs; this is as powerful as a physical addiction, and they then find it impossible to cope with the withdrawal symptoms.

If you suspect your child is taking drugs but won't admit it, look for the following signs: changed behaviour, sleeping a lot, becoming confused or apathetic; you may notice eye droppers, cigarette papers, odd bits of tin foil, empty discarded solvent or hair-spray containers, razor blades with blood on them, scorched metal such as on the basin of a spoon. If your child begins to wear long sleeves it may be to cover-up needle marks. Open denial usually comes from fear. Letting your child know you are not going to blow your top, but want to help, is the only way to overcome this. Remember, it is illegal, so you do have the right to investigate.

There are thousands of drug takers who wish they could stop but do not have the total commitment that it involves. It is similar to being an alcoholic; even ten years after giving up the body will still respond as it did before if he/she tries 'just one drink'. It is therefore very important for people who have stopped taking drugs to change their life style and remove themselves from that environment. It isn't going to be easy to do without something that has been controlling the way they feel. There is real fear of 'coming clean'; some people are terrified at the thought of living without drugs and yet, at the same time, terrified to continue using them. (People on legally prescribed sleeping tablets and tranquillizers often have similar fears.)

When your son or daughter decides to come off drugs they will need outside help. It is unlikely that you will have the skills, ability, or strength to do this alone. It will be tough, it may nearly break your heart, but going along with the drug therapist will help give back your child his/her life. They are going to need compassion and firmness, and will have to find an alternative that gives the lift drugs once did. One man who came to me for help in coming off drugs decided to take up weight training with the aim of making his body as fit as he could – he succeeded in stopping.

Offer support and exercise control but do not accept responsibility. The teenager knew what he was doing; he must now make the choice to cut drugs out of his life completely. The following may help but you will have to be prepared to be involved.

- Moving into a different social environment
- Staying away completely from people whom he knows are on drugs
- Having a companion who is 'clean' and committed to 'being there' with your teenager while he makes the transition
- Giving your teenager *your* time and doing things together. (This may well have to be a total commitment at first – don't start it unless you can follow it through)
- No parties unless you are there to supervise them personally
- Taking up a hobby or activity that occupies his free time – ones that get the adrenaline flowing can produce the same elated feeling that some drugs provide; these need to be mentally creative and/or physically demanding
- Attending a course on relaxation and self-hypnosis

Note: John C Lilly, MD explains in his book, *The Centre of the Cyclone*, how he was able to have the same uplifting and mystical experiences using hypnosis as he had from experimenting with LSD before its dangers were known and it became a controlled drug. Hypnosis is a safe alternative to drugs and leaves the person completely in control. It should, however, be taught by an experienced person.

Take heart; your adolescent is probably so involved in his own interests that there is no way he is going to be led into the drug trap.

A home where they can bring their friends, feel loved and respected, will help. Your example will help too, but then there are always those children who feel they simply *have* to rebel and, for a time at least, need to feel different to the way they see their parents.

GLUES AND SOLVENTS

Although the sale of these is legal, a shopkeeper is supposed to control their sale to people under a certain age, but this is impossible. People can use surgical spirits, methylated spirits, hair spray and a dozen other products that, when inhaled, will change the way they feel. I know of a girl of fourteen who nearly died from sniffing hair spray.

The only way to protect your child is to talk to her and to make her aware of the dangers.

ALCOHOL

Alcohol abuse is on the increase, and at the time of writing is a bigger health problem than drugs. It isn't illegal, and not every-body who drinks is a waster or dropout. Drinking can be thought to be very sophisticated, and many people feel more comfortable with a glass in their hand. Red wine with a meal is now said to reduce heart disease, and a glass of beer in the evening helps us to relax, and reduces stress.

The problem is that our brains all respond differently to alcohol. Some people can take a couple of drinks every night and never become addicted, but others cannot. By the time the latter discover this they find it hard to stop. You cannot persuade anyone to stop drinking unless *they* decide to do so. They will always find a way of hiding their habit.

When teenagers are out with friends, one may encourage another to drink to the point of collapse. Although there is nothing adult about this kind of behaviour, it *seems* grown-up to them. However, most young people have outgrown the need to drink to excess by the time they reach their twenties.

I come into contact with far more women with a drink problem than men. In all cases they are using alcohol as a means of escape from a part of their life that has become intolerable. Although this is not usually true of teenagers, they may start to drink excessively as a way of coping if they fail to develop more mature ways of handling their feelings and dealing with problems.

Teenagers who are drunk should never be laughed at, or encouraged to have one more. It is sad and does nothing to help them. Their self-esteem is probably at rock-bottom already.

When visiting a colleague in hospital I noticed a man in a cot nearby who was going through hell from alcoholic poisoning. The men in the ward thought his behaviour hilarious – but they did not laugh when he died.

CIGARETTES

Some children hate the smell of cigarettes and decide at an early age never to smoke. Others try out of curiosity, because it seems the grown-up thing to do, or to be like their pals. Few people enjoy smoking at first; it is an acquired habit. The argument against smoking is that it does damage your health, is an awful waste of money, is unpleasant for other people and pollutes the air.

Helping your child to decide early on that this is something she will never do is a wise move. The promise of a special present at twenty-one for not smoking can be a great incentive. (Most people who choose to smoke take up the habit before this age.) Schools are now very active in informing children of the health hazards, air pollution, and the anti-social aspects of smoking, but it is still good for you to voice your opinions and explain why you believe smoking is bad. If you know someone who has died from lung cancer or a smoking related disease, a serious chat to close relatives can be very helpful. When someone explains first hand the effect smoking has had on them, it has more impact; they are saying, 'this is for real, it does happen, it happened to us'.

You may like to relate this true story. A man, whose air passages had become blocked with the residue from smoking cigarettes, had to have a hole (a surgical incision) made into his neck (known as a tracheotomy) to enable him to breathe. A friend, visiting him in hospital, was persuaded to light a cigarette and place it against the hole in order that the man could draw smoke into his lungs. He began to cough and choke, his face turned purple – he could no longer breathe. Even though the medical staff were doing their best to help him, he was so addicted to nicotine that he could not stop smoking. He died a few hours later. Dying is a drastic way to discover that smoking is a fool's game.

One very important way of helping your child to a healthy, happy, confident life, is by talking to them about feeling good about themselves; in not having to do what others do. Being in control of their own life and responses means they don't want or need to take any kind of mind or body controlling substances. *They enjoy being themselves.* Demonstrating this yourself is by far the best way of reinforcing well-meaning words.

If your teenager is already smoking you may encourage him to stop, but in order to be successful the decision will have to be his.

You do not have to allow smoking in your house. At one time people found it hard to ask others to comply with this, but following increased health warnings and publicity this is no longer so. Your children's friends should not smoke in your house either, unless you say so!

Smoking, using drugs and drinking, all cost a lot of money. If your adolescent has limited finances he is less likely to squander them, and those peddling drugs are more inclined to leave him alone. If you have already trained him to spend wisely and to feel proud of his ability to balance a budget, this may give him the strength of will to stay away from wasting money on such short-term returns.

10   Starting Work

Many teenagers will not go on to further education in colleges or universities after school. This may be either from choice, or because they do not attain the necessary examination results. Whatever your child decides to do it is important to support him. You may think being a factory worker or stacking shelves in the local supermarket is not what you had planned for him; it may not be what he wants either. All kinds of influences and fears will affect his decision. Having to please you or fulfil your expectations of him should not be an additional pressure.

Some teenagers do not have the confidence to leave home and move away into an unknown part of the country; getting a job that enables them to stay at home seems the safest thing to do. For others, taking up a job for a year or travelling before returning to study could be just what they need. This is one reason why some universities have a 'year out' option. If the job or travel experience isn't as they expected, it is far better to find out early on and have the chance to change direction.

The most important thing is to make further education available to your child and not to criticize him if he decides to go straight into employment, or to take a year out and travel if that is really what he wants to do.

THE BIG MISTAKE

Choosing a career and staying with it for life has really become a thing of the past. Whatever your child decides to do it is unlikely to be a permanent disaster; he can always change direction. I have a friend who started as a carpenter's apprentice; after he married he went back to college and trained as a draftsman. Another began as an engineer and eventually became a teacher.

Try not to panic if your teenager gives the impression that he doesn't care what job he has; the real time to panic is when he doesn't want to work at all. When this happens you should give him an ultimatum: either find a job, or retrain in an area where there are still job opportunities.

There is absolutely no reason why you should be working hard while your child sits at home watching TV or playing computer games all day. This may sound harsh if there appear to be no job opportunities in your area, but that is almost never true – it's just that people don't choose to do them. Take a look at the local newspapers and in the employment offices, see what is available and point your son or daughter in that direction.

Help will be offered while they are still at school and so you may only need to offer support. It is a big mistake to make life too easy for your teenager. If he is determined not to work – *I can live off the dole* – then some positive action must be taken: you make him responsible for running the home, which includes cooking and washing; or he gets work with a local charity; or he takes anything (for the time being) that offers honest payment while he develops other skills that will enable him to move on.

FINDING A JOB

Many people who have started on the 'workshop floor' have ended up in management. Hairdressers start by sweeping up and cleaning down for the stylists; engineers begin by cleaning machines and fetching in bars of steel; the same applies to chefs, landscape designers and supermarket managers. The important thing is to get a foot in the door, at whatever level.

Some young people seem unwilling to take on a job which is not exactly what they want. I noticed a job advertised in our local supermarket for a trainee baker – no previous experience was necessary. At the same time there were youngsters sitting in the street outside with an old hat on the ground and *Please help* scrawled on pieces of cardboard, claiming they had no home and no money. I told several of them about this job; still it remained vacant. When I spoke to the manager he told me that no one would take it because they didn't like the hours. It meant starting at five in the morning and finishing at noon.

Another obstacle is that many people are financially better off being supported on state benefit than by working. This sounds ludicrous, but it is true. We have to find some way of getting our children to understand that this is an appalling way to spend their lives; it lacks purpose, prevents a sense of self-worth, and has to be paid for by those who do work. Most important of all, they will never move forwards.

Your example and attitude will go a long way in encouraging or discouraging your children to get a job. If they hear you always moaning, or see you sitting at home doing nothing all day, they are going to question the wisdom of working for a living.

While your teenager is unemployed, or in what seems like a dead-end job, there is no reason why he cannot attend evening classes and work towards adding some very useful skills to his Curriculum Vitae (CV). Learning another language may lead to him being selected over others in a future job interview.

Taking two jobs when only part-time ones are available is an alternative. Some people I know who do this really enjoy the variety, and wouldn't choose to work any other way.

Where possible, your teenager should be encouraged to select a job that suits his personality. Get him to write a list of all those things he enjoys, or would like to do, irrespective of money, location, education or physical ability. It may look something like this:

- Swimming
- Music
- Children
- TV
- Clothes
- Holidays abroad

Now ask him to consider how he could perhaps incorporate some of those things into earning a living (other subjects on the list will be things he can do in his free time).

Taking the above list as an example, he may decide that he would like to work at a sports centre coaching swimming or working as a life guard. Perhaps he can get a job designing clothes – even starting up his own business. Angela started doing this from home when she couldn't get a job; she now makes the most beautiful wedding dresses and outfits, although she started by altering ready-made clothes for people.

If your son watches a lot of TV and would like to get involved in this area, opportunities are available for young people in 'work experience' schemes; these may not be paid jobs to start with, but I know quite a few who began that way and now have moved on to permanent jobs. One presents his own children's TV show.

Much more attention is paid to those who actually make the effort to call in at the job centre and ask about work than those who just sit at home and fill in endless job applications; it shows you are really interested and that you are prepared to make some effort.

Many firms offer work to young people and then train them on the job. Remember that all is not lost if your teenager failed to get good exam results, or has no qualifications at all. The most important thing is that he does not develop the 'Poor old me!' attitude, or feel that the world owes him something. We all have to earn our rights.

Your teenager will have listened to many people from various walks of life who come into school to explain what their occupation involves and to answer questions. They will have been given advice from careers officers and specialists and, in many cases, offered work experience either during part of their last year in school or in the holidays. So how can you help? It is important to be supportive while not ramming your ideas down their throats. You may accompany them to the local library to do some research on various jobs; you may be able to introduce them to friends who can help or offer constructive advice. Some teenagers will want to be left alone to make up their own minds – you must respect this but show an interest. Let them know that you care about their future and their goals. If you are aware of special talents they have not considered using, suggest they look in that area.

Dan, whose parents had encouraged him to do a business studies course at the local college, found himself completely out of his depth. He was quite miserable when he came to see us and we tried to get him to talk about those things he enjoyed and did naturally well. When I mentioned cooking, his eyes lit up. 'Why not consider training as a chef?' I suggested. He did, and is now working at one of the top hotels in Germany. He enjoys his work so much that when he later visited us, he insisted on cooking a meal for us.

STARTING THE JOB

This is often tougher than expected. Although your son may have spent hours studying at home, he will not have had the continued discipline of *having* to work all day, five days a week. At first, with so much to take in and remember, it can be exhausting.

Getting up and out of the house on time is extremely hard for some people. Your teenager has to learn to do this for himself; you won't always be around to rouse him and place buttered toast in front of him. Good habits incorporated into a working life style from the beginning must become part of the daily routine. Making breakfast, organizing his own transport and preparing a packed lunch should all be things he learns to do for himself.

The workplace can be demanding, and even frightening at first. The young worker has to learn to fit into a role that may be completely new to him. From being one of the oldest at school or college, he is once more treated like a kid. It's humbling, it can be frustrating, and he might need to come home and throw his weight around a bit to give him a sense of being in charge of his own life.

All this will soon settle down into a routine, and you should reap the benefits from having more time to yourself and an added source of income into the household budget; but most important of all, you will begin to converse at a new level, enjoying the new interests and confidences your grown-up child chooses to share with you.

It really will be a revelation to listen to your son telling you things you never knew, or to discover how mature he has become in his thinking. How your teenager relates to people entirely outside your world will also be fascinating. Watching him break away and form a life of his own should make you feel very proud.

At first, the new young wage-earner may be tempted to spend all that he earns – it is quite exhilarating to know that you can buy whatever you choose with *your* money. Those shoes or jacket Mum said were a waste of money can now be purchased. The fact that he may later discover Mum was right is something that shouldn't spoil the unique experience of finding out for himself the most satisfactory ways of spending his money.

11 *When Things Get Out of Hand*

It is perfectly reasonable to expect some rebellious behaviour from your teenager at some stage: his friends will not always meet with your approval, and he may well experiment with smoking and drinking, and try the occasional drug; he may get involved in intimate relationships long before you think he should. You will have to decide how far to let things go before you intervene.

It is possible for any child to get out of hand, stay away from school, break the law, become involved with the wrong crowd or become addicted to drugs. It is important to consider what action is appropriate should your rules and values and/or the law be violated.

The first step is to recognize when things have gone too far. The sooner positive action is taken the better chance you have of success. A formed behaviour or a set habit is harder to break. If you have ever smoked, got into the habit of watching TV every night, or going down to the pub for a drink each day after work, you will know that this is true.

Children get into trouble for all kinds of different reasons – this does not mean that you are a bad parent. Some children are naturally more curious than others, and they simply have to try things for themselves; others are easily led or rebel. Behaviour that is causing major problems may involve a lot of anger and/or be the adolescent's way of making a statement about how he is feeling. There are some youngsters who just drift into problem areas and don't know how to get out again.

Young men are having a particularly tough time in finding

where they belong in today's society. The male has a fundamental need to be the 'head' of his family – the leader, protector and provider – this is how, in times past, we survived. Now, with the new social structure that has evolved, men do not know where they belong and they can feel useless, worthless, and quite desperate to 'prove themselves'. Many are confused and lost. The old motivation has gone, and manly pride no longer seems attainable or even acceptable. Craving the attention and approval of their peers, young males are becoming more destructive and defiant and the whole of our society is suffering as a consequence of this lost 'image' and the need to feel 'macho'. There is an urgent need for this problem to be addressed.

WHAT TO LOOK FOR

Any of the following signs may indicate that something is going seriously wrong with your adolescent's life:

- Becoming secretive and refusing to say where they are going
- Marked changes in their eating habits
- Staying in their rooms and not going out
- Aggressive defiant behaviour
- Frequent truancy from school
- Getting into frequent fights
- Sexual promiscuity
- Anger outbursts
- Violation of the law
- Persistent lying
- Stealing
- Continual state of depression
- Deliberate vandalism

Try talking to your child. Choosing the right moment is essential: you are not going to get co-operation if they have just walked in drunk, or have a date in ten minutes. All communication works best if you do not have to deal with other distractions at the same time.

From the start, let your adolescent know you are concerned for her and not just upset because of the effect her behaviour is having, or might have, on your life. Both parents addressing the problem together helps. You give each other support, and the child knows you both care. And where you need to exercise rules very firmly, they need to know that, as parents, you are both committed to enforcing them.

'You seem so unhappy recently (or angry, confused, with-drawn, upset) we thought that maybe you needed to talk about what's going on.' This may open the door to communication; if it doesn't, then you will have to be more direct: 'Jim, we are very worried (or upset) when you come home drunk, go off with that crowd who we know are on drugs (or whatever). Have you considered what it is doing to your life?'

WHEN THE POLICE BECOME INVOLVED

A police record is going to stay with your child for a long time. Breaking the law is a very serious offence.

A brush with the law can often be all that is needed to shock your teenager out of a downslide in her behaviour. If you have taught her to have a healthy respect for the law this will most certainly help. If she says, 'It's my life, I can do what I like with it', you need to point out that it is also affecting your lives. If she is under age it is also your responsibility. Tell her that none of us can do just as we like.

Theft is the most common problem police have to deal with where teenagers are concerned. They often don't realize quite what they've done until they are caught; they may have seen it as a bit of fun or excitement. That doesn't, of course, make it right. Taking small items that won't be missed or are easy to sell on gives them money to spend; this makes them feel grown-up and in control of their own lives.

Some teenagers steal to draw attention to the fact that they are unhappy, or deeply troubled by something. With others it may be something that the 'gang' do, and to be accepted they have to join in. This can include vandalism or breaking into other people's property for the hell of it.

Most children lie and steal (usually from their parents) when they are little; they should have learned that this is wrong and have stopped by the time they reach their teens. If your child continues to steal or lie, protecting her does more harm than good. Being made to account for her behaviour is the best way of making her realize that she really is responsible for her actions. Don't be tempted to find excuses for her.

More and more people are turning to crime and petty theft to support their drug habit, and this is causing tremendous problems for society and the police. Once a teenager has reached this stage the best thing you can do is to inform the police. This is not betrayal, but the shortest route to ensuring your child receives the help he needs.

Where there is repeated conflict with the law, it is a good idea to let the teenager spend a few hours in the police station; this is going to scare her more than you might imagine. It also gives her time for quiet contemplation.

One of my sons, walking home from town one night with a friend, decided on a whim to remove a road cone. They happened to be seen by a passing policeman and ended up receiving a good telling off at the local police station. This did more to make them careful to stay on the right side of the law than anything I might have said.

UNWANTED PREGNANCY

What do you do when your daughter tells you she is pregnant? The first reaction is usually one of despair: it will ruin her life, you will have to look after the baby, she wants an abortion.

You need to sit down with her and talk about the possible

consequences and options, including adoption. She will also need to make a visit to her doctor as soon as possible. If she wants to keep the baby, then the father may have to be considered in plans for the future. If he doesn't want to know – or even worse, she doesn't know who he is – she is going to need a lot of financial and emotional support from you. A young child coming into the family is probably going to wreck your own long-term plans.

Abortion is now available in more countries than ever before. If this is the chosen option, it will have to be supported on medical and/or emotional grounds. Make sure your daughter is counselled; it is hard to make rational, long-term decisions when faced with such trauma. Many women who decide on abortion or adoption have serious problems coping with this in later life.

An unwanted pregnancy is not evidence that your daughter has been promiscuous or that she even wanted to be sexually involved. She may have felt she *had* to in order to keep her boyfriend. It may have happened while she was drunk. She could have been raped.

RAPE

Many girls (and boys) who have been raped do not report it – or at least, not at first. The shame, disgrace and consequence of letting it be known result in them hiding or denying the experience. Having to be medically examined, appear in court and answer dozens of intimate questions can all cause the victim to hide behind silence. This may result in the girl becoming very withdrawn, depressed and emotional, or treating herself badly as if it were all her fault. There is also the risk of infection. If you suspect that your daughter (or son) has been raped you must take action.

Often the rapist is known to the victim. It may be someone they trusted and even loved. It could be a member of the family which makes it all the harder for the victim to reveal the awful truth.

In all rape cases it is advisable to seek outside help. Many counsellors have been rape victims themselves, and have become counsellors in order to help others. If you don't know where to get help, you can ask at your citizen's advice bureau or your library, look in the telephone directory or pick up a leaflet at your clinic or doctor's surgery. A list of organizations with trained people to help is given at the end of this book. Remember that *you* may need counselling too.

SEXUAL MOLESTATION AND ABUSE

There is no excuse or justification for touching a child in an intimate way. If permission is given by the child that is irrelevant, for many children do not know what is right or wrong – they still have to be taught. Grandad pushing his fingers up the leg of Sarah's knickers to tickle her is wrong; Uncle Fred sticking his tongue in her mouth when he kisses fourteen-year-old Amy is wrong; masturbation involving a child is wrong.

It is important to teach our children as early as possible how to behave in such circumstances and to let them know you will believe them when they tell you something that sounds shocking or unbelievable. Abuse can take many forms and is often difficult to define. Tell your child that if she doesn't like what is happening and/or it offends her, it should not be allowed to continue. I am appalled by the number of boys and girls who have been abused and dared not tell. It is not the fault of the child, however provocative their behaviour.

If your child is sexually abused this should be reported to the authorities. This may sound drastic if the abuser is a close relative, but history shows that these people do not stop until they are found out and made to face up to their crime. Also, they need treatment.

VIOLENT BEHAVIOUR

Children throwing tantrums, smashing your favourite plant, yelling or screaming until they go blue in the face, is not unusual. When they find this behaviour doesn't get the required results it is replaced by something else – this may include tears, sulks or sullen compliance – but eventually they discover that pleasing you is the best way of getting what they want and living in harmony.

A teenager still behaving in a violent manner, on the other hand, should be taken very seriously. He can cause untold damage. If reason does not work and he refuses to listen or consider your feelings, or to respect your property, then you do need to get help. If he is 13 or over and is still deliberately causing damage in the home, don't wait for things to get better – take action. It is unlikely that he will change until he is given counselling and taught to handle his feelings in a better way.

Using a counsellor who is not emotionally involved allows you both to be heard in an impartial way. When your teenager absolutely refuses to talk to someone else, you may choose to speak to someone in his school, or go for counselling yourself. In desperation, many parents tell their children to leave. This may give you peace within the home, but will not help your child to resolve his problem. Let him know when you don't like his present behaviour, but that it doesn't stop you caring for him. Most people do eventually find better ways of handling extreme feelings.

SELF-MUTILATION

When people harm themselves it is because they hate who they are, feel everything is their fault, and believe they need to be punished in some way. If you notice your adolescent is punishing himself, that injuries are appearing on his body for which there is no explanation, that he puts himself in uncomfortable positions and doesn't move for hours, then he is hurting inside and needs help. This may be a way of calling attention to his pain, or it may be a way of punishing you. Whatever the reason, he needs the expert help of either a psychiatrist or psychotherapist.

Some people can only get sexual satisfaction by being hurt and this can be another reason for physical damage that has no apparent explanation. This is abnormal and reveals an underlying problem that needs professional help.

PROBLEMS AT SCHOOL

When you get a phone call from the school complaining about your child's behaviour, take it seriously. As teenagers begin to feel that they can do what they like with their own lives, they may begin to resist being treated like a child at school. They may still attend when it suits them but cause terrible disruption in the class. Teachers are paid to teach and if a pupil is preventing this he will be put in a special class, suspended, or expelled.

If both parents are working all day, they may not have any idea whether their teenager is at school or not.

A working solution has to be found. If it is considered that in the child's best interests he does not stay on at school, you will be told; it may be possible for him to attend a special needs school where smaller classes and specialist teachers will help sort out his problems and still enable him to get an education.

You may be shocked to discover that although your daughter is a model child at home she is behaving very badly in school. Again you need to find out why. Ask to see the school psychologist – they really are very skilled at dealing with teenage problems. You may have to face the fact that something that is happening in the home is responsible for the bad behaviour.

As a therapist, I have dealt with many cases of school phobia. If forced to go, the child can become ill and this may lead to a breakdown where recovery is long and painful. Something is causing that fear, and you must find out what it is. The most frequent reason is fear of a teacher, or bullying. School phobia sometimes happens when a parent dies or one leaves home; the child finds that she cannot cope with the questions or feels alienated by her feelings; she may be afraid to leave the other parent in case something happens to him or her as well.

GAMBLING AND ADDICTIVE BEHAVIOUR

Amusement arcades have been around for more than half a century. Over the past ten years the available games have become more and more sophisticated, incorporating the technology of computerized visual challenges that, in many cases, become addictive.

Many young people are seen using these machines when they should be in school. A frightening number are stealing in order to fund their addictions. They offer promise, a sense of achievement, and with many there is the chance to win small amounts of money. Many feel that by becoming good on these machines they are successful. Sadly, the consequence is often addiction.

One way to avoid this is to give your teenager access to computers, which will help develop useful skills and does not involve parting with money. Many colleges and schools do now make computers available outside of school hours, and there are computer clubs in larger towns and cities. Having a computer in the home is a good investment, particularly now that prices have fallen considerably, and the programmes available are so informative that all the family may benefit by using them.

SUICIDE

You do not have to be neurotic or have a psychiatric history to contemplate suicide: anyone can become so desperate that they consider or attempt it. Some, sadly, succeed.

Threatened or attempted suicide is often a desperate cry for help; it may happen because the person can no longer see an alternative. Adolescents attempt to take their own lives for a number of reasons: worry over exams, bullying, a broken romance, believing they have no future, that they have an incurable disease, feeling they have failed in some way, hating who they are, guilt.

Young people in this state need immediate professional help. Telling them that things will blow over or are not as bad as they seem is masking the problem and delaying getting the help they need, and may depress them even further.

People who are really determined to end their lives rarely mention how they feel; it is therefore useless to take the blame or feel that you ought to have guessed and somehow prevented it.

When you are aware that your adolescent is distressed, is excessively anxious, becomes paranoid, is unable to make decisions, or stops seeing friends, try to find out why. If they can't tell you they may be able to talk to someone outside the family or to a professional counsellor.

EATING DISORDERS

Eating disorders in adolescence – whether anorexia or bulimia – usually start long before one becomes aware that something is wrong. Although it occasionally happens with boys, it is nearly always a problem that comes about when a girl, in some way, feels inadequate, unloved, or believes that changing the way she looks is the only way she will be accepted.

For some girls drastic eating patterns seem to be the only area in which they have control. This is an emotional problem and very hard to change. Girls who virtually give up eating, or who eat and then make themselves vomit or use laxatives, cannot see that what they are doing is harmful.

By depriving themselves of essential vitamins and minerals, anorexics eventually suffer from malnutrition. By the time her physical state indicates this – periods may stop, or there may be bleeding from the nose or mouth – she may become confused and unable to concentrate. She cannot stop what she is doing and is in very serious trouble. This condition can kill. It is very serious and should not be ignored; girls who go along this road need professional help as soon as possible. It is estimated that one in five young women are affected by these potentially life-threatening behaviours. If you are concerned about your child's eating habits do something about it *now*.

Your daughter will need medical help and to be given counselling, psychotherapy and/or psychiatric treatment. No satisfactory way of resolving this problem has yet been found. The best way you can help is to let her know you love her and that you accept her, no matter how she looks. Give her time and *really* listen to what she is saying. It is very important that you do not make a big thing about the way *you* look, or how much you weigh. Neither should you go on and on about her eating habits, although this is hard to stop doing when you are very concerned. *Note:* Specialist books dealing with eating disorders available in the United States and the UK are listed at the end of this book.

YOU ARE NOT ON YOUR OWN

Whatever happens, it is good to remember that others have had similar problems. You are not a failure if you cannot solve every problem on your own. If you could, the experts would be redundant. You may know your child better than anyone else, but an outsider sometimes has the influence or experience that is needed. Don't let shame, guilt, pride, or 'what will grandad think', stop you from getting help for your teenager. It could save her life.

12   Family Problems

DIVORCED AND SINGLE-PARENT FAMILIES

Whether you are a single parent as a result of bereavement, separation or divorce, it is harder when you have to make all the decisions, exercise all the discipline, and try to fill the role of both parents. However, some single parents tell me that this is preferable to the hell they were living in before separation, and that they are now able to offer stability and peace to their children. Reaching a decision to 'go it alone' is something only you can decide.

Often parents actually get on better apart and are able to form a working relationship in which they share the responsibilities and allow the children to move freely between the two homes. Many find this impossible and the children end up feeling that their loyalties are torn; they become confused, angry, hurt and very unhappy.

Jenny was considering leaving her husband. 'We are always quarrelling,' she said. 'It will be better for the children if we separate.' 'There is an alternative,' a friend told her. Jenny expressed suspicion. 'What?' she asked. 'Stop quarrelling and find a solution to your differences.' She did, and it worked. Now the children have grown-up, Jenny and Bill are still together in a relationship that has strengthened, holding memories and experiences they would have missed had they parted.

When we have children we take on a commitment. While

they are young and still dependent we should do all that is possible to make them feel loved and wanted by both parents.

Divorce is not the fault of the child, though many children think it must be because of something they have done. Sharing what is going on with your child can avoid the shock of suddenly discovering that Dad or Mum has gone. But whatever your feelings, do not involve your children in your arguments.

The guilt, anger, anxiety and fears that are part of separation and divorce need to be resolved, but whatever your pain, try to stay tuned-in to your child's feelings. Because your child is a teenager doesn't mean it hurts any less. If he says, 'That's okay by me,' he is probably covering feelings that he does not know how to handle; denying them only pushes the hurt underground. If possible, reassure your child that the parent who moves out still cares very much about him and that the problem is the parents', and not his.

Some children who are very unhappy in the midst of parental conflict will actually run away in the hope that it will bring the parents to their senses. 'I just want everything to be as it was,' is a plaintive cry from the heart.

It is not beyond a child to play one parent off against the other. After a row at home they may decide to go and live with the other parent. This is often an excellent idea and it usually isn't long before they return home, having decided the freedom they envisaged does not come up to their expectations.

If your teenager flounces off after a row, make it clear that you still love him and that he can come home when he wishes. Most who rush off in temper, or because they are feeling hurt, regret it within days. But it is hard to climb down and admit you made a mistake. The return should not be heralded with angry words. A 'Good, you're back. Would you like omelettes for tea, or have you eaten?' or something similar will tell him everything's all right. Later, you may like to ask if he wants to talk about what happened and see if you can help sort things out.

Above all else you are both still the parents of your child and it is your responsibility to provide a solid foundation. You should present a united front no matter what you think about each other in private. Telling your child that his father is a slob or drunk, and *For heaven's sake don't grow up to be like him*, isn't going to help. Dad may have faults but instead of highlighting them, help keep your son's focus on his good points. Surprisingly, you may find the father starts to do all kind of things with his son (or daughter) that he never offered to do when you lived together. Welcome it; don't knock it with sarcasm.

Prearranged times when each of you will have the children sounds like a practical solution to sharing the responsibility. It gives each of you some time to yourself or to spend with a new partner or friend. In reality it is not so simple. When a father, for example, has his children every other weekend, he feels he has to give them that time. But what do you do with two children for forty-eight hours? If they have reached teenage they would, under normal conditions, be spending time out with their friends or pursuing their own pastimes.

Try to include them in your life when you do have them. They may help in the garden, go shopping with you, walk the dog and cook dinner, but as they grow older they are going to miss their own life style. You probably need time to yourself after a week at work and can feel frustrated at not being able to get on with things, or just unwind. By working out a day, or weekend, that is acceptable to both you and your children, this strain can be avoided.

Eventually your children will make it clear that they don't want to spend so much time with you. Don't feel rejected; this would happen if you were still all living together. Let them go, knowing they are now old enough to get in touch and come to see you when they choose to do so.

NO DAD AT ALL

Some children never know their father, and can feel deprived and angry because they are seen as 'different'. When all the other children have parents visiting school on special occasions, when other Dads are there watching their sons play football, when friends talk about family outings, the child *is* going to feel left out or different.

You will have made a conscious decision at the start to keep your baby, but as the child grows and things change, you will probably discover that you need outside help. It is okay to ask for help, especially when your teenager demonstrates his or her need for the other parent. Relatives or a good friend may be really glad to fill his role. Emphasize to your child how much he or she was and is wanted. One of the advantages of this situation becoming more common is that it is no longer seen as a stigma and the child is less likely to be teased or bullied because of it.

A NEW PARENT IN THE FAMILY

Someone moving in, seemingly taking over Dad's or Mum's role, is likely to have a hard time at first. The child will usually feel resentful and will behave quite badly.

A boy was brought to see me who set about taking on the role of the man of the house after his father left home. He was twelve years old and would not let his mother have any life that did not include him. I asked him how he felt when he went off with *his* friends. 'That's different,' he replied. 'Mum doesn't need anybody else, she's got me.'

It is best for a new parent not to try and play the role of father (or mother), but to develop a position of his own – usually somewhere between a loved uncle and a friend. In an argument the child is quite likely to retaliate with, 'You're not my Dad anyhow!'

I know of one man in his forties, who now confesses to doing everything he could to separate his father from his new wife, even though his parents had divorced several years earlier. 'I

Many young people eventually see the new parent as someone special

wanted my Dad to myself when I went to visit him,' he said. 'I must have given her hell.' Since his father died, he has come to realize that he is really quite fond of the second wife, and now he chooses to visit her and help her.

Many adults who behaved really badly during their teens, now see the partner of their parent as actually being someone special, and they wonder why they put up with their abominable behaviour when they were younger. You have to have a lot of love, courage and understanding to hold on and wait for this realization to unfold.

Your behaviour and feelings do have a profound effect upon your teenager. Just when he is going through heightened feelings of falling in love and sexual awakening, he finds his Mum or Dad has a lover, or may be contemplating marriage to someone he sees as an intruder.

It is wise to protect your child from your own sexual activities.

This is one time where modesty, or playing down your feelings, is the kindest way of letting your adolescent have centre stage for his own feelings. Walking into the bedroom and finding Mum in bed with a bloke he hardly knows is not going to help him come to accept a long-term future relationship you may be planning. And although Dad may have moved out ages ago, even remarried, the son (or daughter) may still see the new man as someone trying to take his place. Using sensitive behaviour is not deceitful but is a mature way of dealing with an age-old problem – your teenager does not want to have to compete with anyone for you.

STEP-CHILDREN

Your partner's children arrive on Friday. How do you feel? They would probably be astounded to know that you are nervous, if not downright terrified. They will already have met you, have been on outings that included you, but now you are married to their Dad (or Mum) and you are going to start telling them what to do. And of course, sometimes you will have to; leaving all discipline and decisions to their blood parent does not help create a united front, and will make the child (or children) aware that *you* don't really belong in *their* family.

The teenager has a very real need to still feel particularly special to the blood parent; making sure that she can still have Mum or Dad to herself some of the time is important. This also gives you space to pursue interests of your own which will help you maintain your own identity.

If you each have children they are going to have to learn to mix. Often they are better at doing this than you realize. There will most likely be some rivalry and jealousy, but then there is between brothers and sisters. By making no concessions and not treating them any differently to your own children, the step-children will find it easier to settle down.

Do show that you care. One woman I know tells me that after her mother died and father remarried she was never hugged or kissed again. The step-mother was so insecure she couldn't cope with the father showing affection to his children, and she didn't know how to love them.

BEREAVEMENT

To lose a parent is devastating. Often so much attention is being given to the surviving spouse at the time that the children go unnoticed. You may not be in a state to give your children solace or assurance at this time. The finality of death is frightening. The safe secure world they have lived in has been turned upside down. They may experience feelings of guilt; in an irrational way they may convince themselves that it would not have happened had they been a better son, or daughter. Filled with remorse, they tell themselves that they would have spent more time at home if they had known Mum or Dad was going to die.

If you are unable to offer the comfort your children need, ask a close relative or friend to make sure they have someone they can talk to, someone they can go to at any time of the day or night. We do get over things in time, but it is hard to know this when you are sixteen.

The loss of a sibling is another critical time. Tanya, who had a baby brother whom she adored, was never told when he died. When she asked where he was (she was four at the time), she was told not to speak about it because it would upset Mummy. She spent years living with the unknown, wondering if she was responsible. When she came to me as a client she had been labelled a manic depressive. By using regressive hypnosis she was able to deal with her bereavement and come to terms with her loss. She then went on to sort out her marriage, and now has two lovely children.

SHARING THE PROBLEM

Parental problems do affect the rest of the family even though your teenager may behave as if she couldn't care less. If you are having money worries, are concerned about an elderly relative, your partner has become alcoholic, or you are about to be made redundant, don't keep your problems in the dark. Sharing can make them feel very mature, and they may surprise you by offering constructive advice or help.

WHEN A GRANDPARENT MOVES IN

The arrival of a grandparent who can no longer cope on his/her own is going to affect all the family. By discussing this with them and then working out how things can best be arranged, you will avoid some of the problems – though not all.

Older people, without realizing it, can put a terrible burden on a family. I also believe that if they can be integrated into the family and are loving and considerate, then everyone can benefit from the new arrangement. Young people discover they have a confidant who is usually on their side; grandparents have the time to make us feel special, whatever our age.

It is essential from the start to explain to the grandparent that disciplining the children is your job. They had their go at doing this when you were a child; now is the time for them to sit back and simply enjoy being a grandparent. This isn't as easy as it sounds. Because values, life styles, and what is considered acceptable do change with each generation, it may be hard for granny not to frown from time to time and warn you that, 'Sophie will come to no good wearing clothes like that!' She will have forgotten that her mother most probably said the same thing to her seventy years before.

Some houses can be adapted to allow the older person space of their own. Where this isn't possible, you will have to consider the rest of the family and their rights before – however much you care – you take in another person on a permanent basis.

Teenagers need space. They also need to play modern music (usually loudly), to stay up late, entertain their friends, and not be told on a regular basis what it was like in granny's day.

Should the grandparent be a querulous, complaining, negative person, you really are probably quite right in insisting that other arrangements are made. A miserable old person sitting in the armchair every time your teenager walks into the room will only drive her away. You might find you want to leave too!

13 Beliefs, Traditions, Values and Cultures

We live in a changing world. Sometimes this seems for the better, and sometimes we see it as threatening all that we hold dear. One of the most dramatic changes over the pasty fifty years has been in the treatment of women, which is extremely difficult for some cultures and religions to accept. It is also often seen as a threat to the position of men in society. We cannot stop change, but we can explain to our children why we think certain things are not good and why we refuse to support them.

Many countries are becoming multi-cultural, which has put a great burden upon parents with different traditions and beliefs living in a foreign country. Even in Western civilization there is still much controversy over freedom of sex, abortion and contraception.

Afraid of the effect of alien beliefs and customs, many ethnic groups of people are demanding their own churches and schools. This is understandable, but isolation from the rest of the nation is neither practical nor helpful to our young. They need to mix and integrate and yet, at the same time, not feel uncomfortable or rebellious over the differences.

We are tribal at heart, and this is part of our self-protection; when we feel threatened we become aggressive or defensive. Separation is not the way forward; we need greater understanding of each other's beliefs and customs.

When your teenager confronts you and questions your beliefs, you will do well to have seriously considered them beforehand.

Although keeping the head covered may seem essential to modesty, or a turban is worn as part of your religious discipline, if you choose to live in a foreign country you will need to consider whether this is going to cause your child more problems. Separating them from other students in this way can make them want to rebel, or even reject their religion completely. Also, the law of the country in which you reside may force some changes. Crash helmets have to be worn while riding a motorbike in some countries, and soon it is very likely that children will have to wear similar protection when riding a bicycle on the road.

The best way to guide your child is by example. They may stop going to mass when they get to university but are very likely to return to the practices they were taught when they start a serious romance or grow out of the rebellious stage.

In almost all religions we are taught that we do not have the right to judge others – that only God, Allah, Jehovah, Buddha (or whatever name we give to our god) has that right.

Tyrannical control is wrong. No one should be forced to submit to another. If something is right it will prevail. Fear is not the key to discipline, although at times it seems like the shortest route. Understanding gets a more positive response.

Rebellion results from parents having little contact with the outside world. We have seen that lack of understanding and intolerance of other beliefs cause war in many countries. By learning to accept that our neighbour has every right to his own beliefs, and by being kind and respectful, conflicts can be avoided.

It is those teenagers who feel seriously disadvantaged who are most likely to break the law and turn into delinquents. The more we integrate the less likely this is to happen.

We do feel safer with our own kind; it gives us power to be one of many. If this feeling can spread across whole nations, no matter what colour skin, shape of the face, clothes, customs or religious beliefs, then we would become strong, and fear would no longer be at the heart of man.

Most people now see arranged marriages as wrong, and yet many of us unconsciously encourage our sons and daughters towards someone we see as a 'suitable' partner. The powerful movement for human rights is changing many customs and ways of behaviour; in some areas this is going to force change, even challenging religious beliefs. Before we condemn our children for wanting to change things and to copy the ways of other teenagers in the community, we need to listen to them and then tell them why we think our beliefs should be upheld.

Young people are idealistic. New cults can have a great attraction for those who are searching for their own meaning in life. It is a good idea to try to direct their idealism and zeal into productive action. Movements that help the underprivileged, disabled, lonely, the elderly, or which help people of different nations to mix, can be of great benefit to all mankind.

Your beliefs will not always be accepted by your children but they should, if you have thought them out, be respected.

Truth is something we all have to discover in our personal journey through life.

14 Leaving Home

Whether your child leaves home in order to get a job, enter college or university, or to get married, most choose to leave the nest sooner or later. This is the first real test of whether they can survive on their own. Unless your child is prepared, the sheer effort of managing her personal affairs can be overwhelming. A surprising number of students simply don't make it at university because they are unable to cope away from home.

One former student told me that during his first week (he was accommodated within the university building), he walked along the landing knocking on a few doors in the hope of finding someone who would join him to go down to the canteen. He discovered one boy contemplating suicide, and another was packing up having decided to return home already. We once offered accommodation to the daughter of a friend who was moving into the area to attend art college. After five days she came to talk to us: 'I hate it,' she confessed. 'I just don't fit in and the course is not at all as I had expected.' She did, however, enjoy her independence and living away from home. We agreed that she could stay, and she left college and got a job that enabled her to follow her chosen career in design and advertising.

Most will make it, and thoroughly enjoy the new challenges. They will learn how to handle freedom, limited money, the subject they have chosen to study, mixing with a large variety of people, controlling their eating habits, coping with emotional ups and downs and the unpredictable surges of hormones. At home, they should also have developed the skills that enable them to survive – if they have, you have done your job well, so don't feel too upset if at first they don't write home often, and prefer to go off camping with new friends when they get their first break.

Whatever your adult child now decides to do, he has left home and it really is none of your business unless he chooses to share it with you. Usually they do, for at heart most teenagers still need parental approval and psychological support. Feeling ill is one time when most will wish they were back home with Mum to serve up the medicine and make hot drinks. Don't be tempted to rush off and bring them home; this is part of breaking away and learning to survive without you. Obviously, if the illness is serious you will take some action.

Early marriages are often doomed to failure because of parental interference. You may feel that the couple are much too young to know what they are doing or to make their own decisions. If they are old enough to make the commitment to marriage you have to credit them with being able to sort out their own lives. When they ask for help or advice you may get involved with that specific problem, but that is not an open invitation to interfere with other aspects of their life. Money may be a problem; helping out is instinctive, but can undermine their independence and breed resentment. The best way is to show that you still love them and care for their happiness; bale them out once if you feel that is justified and then leave them to get on with their life in their own way.

We try to protect our children by urging them not to marry young, but for some it works very well. If they plan to see something of the world together before settling down in a job, being married gives them mutual support, security and companionship.

Many young people set up home with their lovers with no serious intention of getting married or making a lifetime commitment. You may condone this, ignore that it is happening, or campaign actively against this situation. They will do what they want in the end, and so it is better to stay friends than to create barriers. Parents who only welcome home the son, and not his girlfriend, force him to make extremely hard choices.

Any young couple who decide to marry or live together need privacy. Living in either parents' home is not the best way of starting off in such a relationship, even if, from a financial viewpoint, this seems like the sensible thing to do. Finding somewhere to live and saving up the deposit helps to make them aware of their new responsibilities.

MOVING OUT

As soon as your child is of age, or before if you agree, she will most likely want to move out. It is as well to expect this, and to try and understand, instead of getting hurt and feeling rejected, or that you are a failure. Hold on to the thought that wanting to leave home is normal.

A daughter who is made to feel guilty about leaving home may still go but find it hard to communicate honestly afterwards. However miserable she may feel, she isn't going to admit it to you. You may be able to help by occasionally asking how she feels about leaving home.

After the death of my husband I was sitting one day with my fourth son, who still lived at home, and found myself asking: 'Do you feel ready to leave home, son?' His answer shocked me: 'Yes, but I don't think you are ready to cope without me yet.' I had no idea he thought that way. I made an instant decision to make sure he could leave and that he went with my blessing, assured that I was going to be all right.

Some teenagers are so desperate to get away from home that they end up penniless living on the streets. If parents are arguing all the time, make impossible demands, or the young person is being abused in some way, he will feel driven to leave. Young people who are on drugs often need to join those who support their habit and will leave home to live together with other addicts.

Surprisingly, there are those who enjoy living on the streets. I heard a young woman being interviewed who said she had been given a council flat but felt so lonely and isolated that she chose to return to living rough. 'At least everyone out there is your friend,' she said.

RUNAWAYS

Teenagers who walk out without planning their move first don't usually go far. Often they find a friend who lets them sleep on the couch for a couple of nights before they return home. This is naturally going to cause you worry, and could start a chain of thought that leads you to despair.

Knowing your teenager's friends, and who is most likely to offer her a bed, means you can ring up and check everything is alright. The friend may not feel she can tell you everything she knows but she should be able to tell you that your daughter is okay.

A runaway usually returns home when her clothes or money run out. Don't crow over it. A hug and 'It's nice to have you back', then letting the subject drop, is probably the best way of dealing with the situation.

The following check list has been compiled by teenagers who have left home for a variety of reasons, including attending university. Your own child may find it useful.

- Make sure you have somewhere to go.
- Work out how much money you have to spend and learn to budget (if you buy CDs and then have to go without food for a couple of days that's your lookout).
- If you have a grant, or an allowance, don't spend it in the first week.
- Learn to know how much you can safely drink, and stick to it.

- Try to make friends.
- Join clubs or societies.
- If you're at university or college plan your time and make sure you get your work done (it is very hard to catch up if you fall behind).
- Decide what your priorities are – you do have to sleep some of the time!
- Don't get involved in sex unless you are prepared.
- Walking and cycling is cheaper than public transport; running your own car will mean you end up driving everyone else around.
- It's okay to feel depressed and homesick sometimes – most of us do, though we don't admit it.
- Remember there are a lot of people living away from home who have similar problems to yours.
- Call home occasionally.

15   *Letting* Go

You have been practising this for years: from the moment you let go of your child's hand and he made his first steps alone you were training him to survive without you. You can probably recall how proud you felt. Now you have reached the stage of recognizing your child is an adult, and that means the complete letting go of something you have worked so hard to produce: a mature, responsible, independent human being, capable of running his own life.

There may have been moments when you longed for this time. 'Won't it be wonderful when they don't need us any more? Imagine having the house to ourselves again!' This is, for you as well as your child, a new beginning. You need now to learn to enjoy it.

Some people say we don't ever really grow up until we leave home. There is a lot of truth in this; mothers in particular find it hard not to go on giving just that little bit of advice, or washing that particular shirt they know is going to be needed tomorrow.

If your child is still living at home and has reached the age of 18, I would suggest it is high time he took over total responsibility for his own life. It could be seen as a celebration; you could go out for a meal together and agree on what this entails.

- You will stop giving advice unless it is asked for.
- You will expect him to take his share of work in the kitchen,

which includes making the meal for you once or twice a week.

- You will not enter his room at any time without invitation.
- You will stop criticizing and making sarcastic remarks about his dress or friends.
- You will respect each other's rights to privacy and allow your adult son (or daughter) to keep personal aspects of his life to himself, should he wish to do so.

Well, you work it out together.

FATHER'S POSITION

It isn't easy. A father often finds, particularly with his first son, that he feels let down when his son does not fulfil his expectations. There is a natural rivalry (as in the animal kingdom, of which we are part), but this should not make the father feel inadequate or that he has to defend his authority. Sport is a great leveller in this particular relationship: it is such a wonderful way of releasing energy, building the foundation of a good friendship, engaging in healthy competition, and helping to stay fit that it is a pity so many people see it as something you only do when you are at school, and this applies to girls as much as to boys.

As men grow older they begin to recognize that there are things they can't do so well any more, and this realization may be accompanied by feelings of fear. There may be pressures at work: younger men who are better qualified, the threat of redundancies, the management talking about retiring some of the staff early at 45! Absorbed in his job, often the father only comes to regret the time they might have spent together after his son has left home. He may then become a doting grandfather to his son's amazement, who says, 'You never did any of those things with me!'

When the father–son relationship hits a bad patch, there may be open confrontation, or the 'brick wall' act. Whatever your son is trying to tell you, and however sensible you both are about letting go and getting on with your own lives, your son still needs your love, friendship and approval.

Daniel stopped writing home because, he said, his father dictated letters to his secretary and then had her type them and send them to him. 'He can't even be bothered to write himself,' he told me.

One father used to get furious when he spoke with his son and was met with what he interpreted as a sarcastic smirk. It took a long time before he came to realize it was the nervous reaction of a bewildered teenager who didn't know how to communicate his feelings.

The fears a father feels for his daughter are different. He wants to safeguard her against all men who are likely to misuse her, misinterpret her actions, break her heart. There may also be feelings of jealousy and rejection. It is hard to recognize that a daughter needs just as much reassurance from her father as from her mother. A few words of praise go a long way, whereas criticism rarely results in any positive feelings or action.

'But suppose she goes and does something stupid and gets herself pregnant?' Fear is clouding his ability to think straight: pregnancy isn't the end of the world. It does not have to spoil the rest of her life or ruin a career. Of course, it would be better if it wasn't an accident. Teenage pregnancies are not as frequent as the media suggest, but if this does happen, it is important for the daughter to know that *both* her parents still love her.

Marriage is sometimes used as an act of defiance, or because it is seen as the only way of escape. With foresight and love, this should never be the case with your daughter or son.

Little girls begin to practise their feminine charms on their fathers at a very early age. Those who grow up without a man in the family miss out on this aspect of life and it is a loss. The safest way to find out about men is through contact and by communicating with father – the one who loves you and whom you can entirely trust to have your best interests at heart. This flirting that a daughter uses with her father is part of discovering herself.

It should never be seen as anything more than a natural development that will lead eventually to a heterosexual relationship with a man of her choice.

To stop your son or daughter from demonstrating affection because you consider they are too old for hugs and kisses is a sad reflection of your values and lack of understanding. Many men feel embarrassed to give their sons a hug – they shouldn't. It doesn't mean they have turned soft, or that their sons will become homosexuals. The *lack* of love demonstrated by a father is far more likely to send a son searching for the love of another man.

MOTHER'S POSITION

Where a mother has a good relationship with her son and does not try to control or manipulate him, she will have given him invaluable help in choosing a partner, having the confidence to date a girl, and in avoiding hang-ups over women.

In our society it is still usually the boy who approaches the girl, which is more difficult than one might imagine. Although it gets easier with practice, I still know of a number of young men who are just too shy to ask a girl out. If your son has attended a co-educational school, girls won't seem quite so remote, and he should be able to converse with them without feeling embarrassed.

Resist teasing or making pointed comments when he is obviously going out on a date; it is neither kind nor helpful.

Mothers and daughters are either opposed and can experience tremendous confrontation, or can be really close and act more like girlfriends. This sounds nice, but your daughter needs to know that you hold a position in her life that is different from her friends; she can then use this unique relationship when she feels the need for support and comfort. She must carve her own future and build her own dreams.

READY TO LET GO?

So are you now ready to let go and begin to live your own life again? Having your own interests, a job, friends, something new to get involved in, will all help make this easier.

Being really busy won't leave too much time to worry about how your son or daughter is getting along without you. There are times when I have forgotten to phone mine because I have been so involved in something else. This isn't an indication that I don't care, but is part of recognizing that their need for me has diminished.

Parents and children must grow apart for the simple reason that you are not always going to be here. It is also important that you do not feel as if you have become redundant and that your life is over.

It is a curious fact that although your children will leave home, and perhaps even decide to go and live on the other side of the globe, if *you* do the leaving they feel you have deserted them. They like to know that you will always be available, wherever they are. Letting go is a two-way thing. Perhaps you have always wanted to travel or retire to a warm country; you should not feel that you cannot go because your children expect you to still be there for them.

Whenever you find yourself trying to pull your children back – and this can be done in all sorts of subtle ways – question your intentions. Do you really want them to come round because you are cooking their favourite meal, because Aunt Sue is coming and would love to see them, or that you have a lot of spare vegetables from the garden and you thought they could use them – or is it a way of making sure they come home often because *you* need to see them?

You aren't going to lose your children because you have let go. You still have a place in their lives, and there will still be things they want to share with you; from time to time there will be things you can do together as a family. A new relationship emerges that will make you immensely proud and glad that you

It's hard sometimes to let go

had children. For many, the added bonus of grandchildren is one of the greatest benefits of having been parents.

My eldest son summed up the situation for me one day. We were standing in the garden looking at the flower beds which I had made and he was admiring. 'Now you are all grown-up you no longer need me,' I said. He looked at me surprised, and then told me, 'We do, Mum. You are our anchor.'

Tips For Your Survival

1 Rebellion is part of growing up; if it's not too serious, let it happen.
2 As parents, show a united front.
3 Be consistent.
4 Recognize when you are being manipulated, and stand firm.
5 When you are met with confrontation, pause and question your intention.
6 Challenge unacceptable behaviour – for their own good, adolescents have to learn to live within the structure built by society.
7 Family conflict is normal – stay cool; it will probably be forgotten by morning.
8 Don't panic; the influence of peers rarely outweighs the values you have given to your child. You can't go on protecting him/her forever.
9 Show an interest in your teenager's life and plans for the future, but don't force your ideas on him.
10 Moods are normal – unless they are prolonged, ignore them. Teenagers enjoy being miserable sometimes.
11 Be aware of your own negative expectations, and learn to trust your child unless proven wrong.
12 Success is in who they become, and not only in what they achieve.
13 Don't be afraid to ask for outside help – the experts do sometimes have skills that you have yet to learn.

14 Treat every child as an individual – their needs and behaviour will differ.
15 Don't be too hard on the first child – this is where you do your learning, so take it easy.
16 Show approval and offer praise whenever the opportunity arises – it is more constructive than criticism.
17 Treat your child with courtesy and respect – remember we learn best by example.
18 Don't be too quick to bale them out of trouble – they have to learn to take responsibility for their own actions.
19 Don't lend money you can't afford to lose.
20 Develop interests of your own.
21 Have fun and enjoy watching your teenagers discover who they are and how they set about building their own future.

Don't treat your teenager like a child!

Organizations Offering Advice and Support

Using your telephone directory you can find the number to any of the following organizations who are there to help and advise you. If the organization is not listed in your area you can obtain the number of its head office through the telephone operator or your Citizen's Advice Bureau.

Australia

Alcohol and Drug Abuse
Alcohol & Drug Information Service
Alcoholics Anonymous

Cults
Centacare

Eating Disorders
Anorexia Nervosa Society
Overeaters Anonymous

Gambling
Gambling Anonymous
 Lifeline

HIV & AIDS
AIDS Council

Homosexuality
Gay Counselling Service
Gay Crisis Network

Missing Persons
Red Cross
The Salvation Army

Pregnancy
Childbirth Education Association
Pregnancy Support Centre

Rape
Lifeline
Rape Crisis Centre

Young People
Distress Call
Kid's Helpline
Youth Emergency Centre

General Counselling
Community Health Centre
Crisis Care
Distress Call
Domestic Violence
Lifeline

Canada

Alcohol Abuse
Al-Anon
Ala-teens

Drug Abuse
Addiction Research Foundation
Narcotics Anonymous

Eating Disorders
Overeaters Anonymous

Gambling
Gamblers Anonymous

HIV & AIDS
AIDS Hotline
National AIDS Clearing House Information

Homosexuality
Lesbian & Gay Youth, Toronto

Pregnancy & Abortion
Birthright

Rape & Sexual Abuse
Communications and Public Affairs
Contact local Sexual Assault Support Centres

General information for residents in Canada
The National Clearing House (tel:1800 2671291) will always put you in touch with an organization who will help with your problem
Contact **Local Crisis Lines** for help and advice with any crisis
Any Government Clinic
Institute of Family Therapy
CLSC Clinic, Quebec, offers a first line contact

South Africa

General Counselling and Advice
Compassionate Friends
South African Federation for Mental Health

United Kingdom

Alcohol Abuse
Accept National Services
Alcohol Concern
Families Anon (help for families of drug users)

Bereavement
CRUSE – offers help and support with bereavement

Cults
Family Action, Information & Rescue

Drug Abuse
Families Anonymous
National Campaign against Solvent Abuse
Release – help with drug and abortion problems

Eating Disorders
Anorexia & Bulimia Nervosa Association

Family Problems
Social Services Department

Gambling
Gambling Anonymous

HIV, AIDS, & Sexually Transmitted Disease
National AIDS Helpline
Terrence Higgins Trust and Body Positive
Look under VD or contact your local hospital

Homosexuality
Acceptance Helpline for Parents
Parents' Friend

MIND (help with mental disorders)

Missing Persons
Missing Persons Bureau
The Salvation Army

One Parent Families
Gingerbread
National Stepfamily Association

Pregnancy
British Pregnancy Advisory Service
Brook Advisory Centres (specialists in birth control for young people)
Family Planning Association

Rape
Incest Crisis Line
Rape Crisis Centre (London)

General Counselling and Advice
Children's Legal Centre (offer advice on law affecting young people)
Institute of Family Therapy
National Association of Citizens Advice Bureaux (offer help and advice on any subject)
Relate
Samaritans
Youth Access

Education
Advisory Centre on Education

British Dyslexia Association
ISIS (Independent Schools Information Service)
National Association for Gifted Children
National Council for Special Education

United States of America

National Hotline Telephone Numbers
AIDS Action National Hotline 1800-342-2437
Al-Anon/Alateen 1800-344-2666
Childhelp USA 1800-422-4453
Gay & Lesbian Adolescent Social Services 1310-358-8727
Literacy Hotline Contact Center 1800-228-8813
National Child Abuse Hotline 1800-422-4453
National Drug Abuse Hotline 1800-662-4357
National Eating Disorders Association 1918-481-4092
National Sexually Transmitted Disease Hotline 1800-227-8922

General Information
See Self-help Guides in local telephone directories

Recommended Reading

By Wendy Grant

Are You In Control? Element Books Ltd, 1995.
Dare! Element Books Ltd, 1995.

Other books include

Buckroyd, Julia, *Anorexia & Bulimia*, Element Books Ltd, 1995.
Coleman, John C, *Teenagers and Sexuality*, Headway, 1995.
Cook, Marion, *Looking Good*, NC Press Ltd, Canada, 1992.
Teenagers and eating disorders.
Cook, Marion, *Please, Listen to Me!* Self-Counsel Publishers, 1993.
A guide to understanding teenagers and suicide.
Hodson, Phillip, *Growing Pains*, BBC Publications, 1988.
A collection of letters from teenagers with responses by the author.
Kriegsman, Kay H, *Taking Charge*, Woodbine House, USA, 1992.
Teenagers talk about life and physical disabilities.
Maqswood, Ruqaiyyah Waris, *Living with Teenagers*, IA-HA Publishers Ltd, 1995.
A guide for Muslim parents.
Nelson, Judith C, *Positive Discipline for Teenagers*, Prima Publishing, USA, 1994.
Phillips, Dan, *Gem of the First Water*, Resource Publications, USA, 1990.
A recovery process for troubled teenagers.

Sheehan, Elaine, *Anxiety, Phobias & Panic Attacks*, Element Books Ltd, 1995.

Skynner, Robin, & Cleese, John, *Families and How to Survive Them*, Penguin, 1983.

Stones, Rosemary, *Loving Encounters*, Piccadilly Publishers, 1988, 1989. A book about sex for teenagers.

Zagdanski, Doris, *Something I've Never Felt Before*, Hill of Content Publishing Co, Australia, 1994. Teenagers coping with grief.

Index